MW01282908

1,000 to 1!

CLAIMING, BREEDING AND RACING THOROUGHBREDS ON A SHOESTRING-AND BEATING THE ODDS

Malcolm Barr, Sr.
with Tom Ardies

Bloomington, IN Milton Keynes, UK

AuthorHouse™
1663 Liberty Drive, Suite 200
Bloomington, IN 47403
www.authorhouse.com
Phone: 1-800-839-8640

AuthorHouse™ UK Ltd.
500 Avebury Boulevard
Central Milton Keynes, MK9 2BE
www.authorhouse.co.uk
Phone: 08001974150

© 2006 Malcolm Barr, Sr. with Tom Ardies. All rights reserved.

*No part of this book may be reproduced, stored in
a retrieval system, or transmitted by any means
without the written permission of the author.*

First published by AuthorHouse 10/10/2006

ISBN: 1-4259-5583-5 (sc)

Printed in the United States of America
Bloomington, Indiana

This book is printed on acid-free paper.

Cover credit: Ellen R. Piazza

For Larry Lacey

People said he might be the only used car salesman to ever get to heaven - and wouldn't that be nice if it were true?

God forbid that I should go to any heaven in which there are no horses.

    - Letter to Theodore Roosevelt from Robert B. Cunningham-Graham

FOREWORD

I have trained more than 120 horses for Malcolm Barr's and Bill Joyce's Hampshire racing partnerships since 1989, and they tell me that more than 100 of their horses have won races. While Malcolm's book gives me and my staff a lot of the credit, the partnership's successes on the track are due in no small part to the management style of the Hampshire, and the ability of Malcolm and his crew to continue to attract many investors into thoroughbred ownership over a great number of years. The Hampshire's longevity in this business never ceases to surprise those of us who have watched similar operations suddenly appear, then disappear just as quickly.

This is not one of the many "how to" books about syndicating horses. Rather, it is about the horses themselves, and the people around the horses, and the people Malcolm and Bill have invited into their partnerships - an interesting and diverse group, to say the least! Malcolm has always found the backside a fascinating place to be, and we've always been pleased to have him around. For one thing, he's one of those rare folk who goes to great lengths not to get in the way, and also, he is an even rarer owner who let's the trainer do his job with minimal interference from himself and from the partners he brings into the game.

The Maryland horse industry should be indebted to Malcolm and Bill for the several hundred people they have brought into race horse ownership. Many of them had never before been to a race track, never mind been close to a horse. They also have been able to keep their partnerships "affordable" to many who would not otherwise have been able to "own" a race horse. They have done this by taking very little for themselves, foregoing the usual management fees and the like in order to conserve investors' cash for the care and upkeep and training of the Hampshire horses. Their efforts to place the injured and just plain tired horses into caring homes as their careers end also are to be commended.

The Hampshire is one of my oldest clients. It's been a pleasure to train horses for them. I hope they will be around another 17 years and allow me to continue to bring them the excitement and, yes, the disappointments, that are all part of this wonderful business of thoroughbred horse racing.

Dale Capuano
Trainer

PROLOGUE

The Tax Reform Code of 1986, for all the good it may have achieved, sounded a virtual death knell for individual ownership of thoroughbred race horses in this country.

Investment in horses, both for racing and breeding, is so uncertain, so speculative, that without liberal write-offs and generous depreciation allowances only the very rich can afford to go it alone.

Joint ownership is, however, a feasible alternative for those of us with modest discretionary funds, and limited partnerships, or syndicates, have been steadily gaining in popularity on a trail blazed in the early 1970s by South Carolina horseman Cot Campbell.

Many of these syndications are informal affairs involving a handful of friends who create a pot to purchase a single horse. Others range from multimillion dollar operations to the more modest arrangements typified by the Hampshire Alliance, Inc., popularly known as the Hampshire racing partnerships.

Like any day at the track, you'll find winners and losers in syndicates. The Hampshire, happily, is, for the most part, one of the winners, and I trust you will enjoy - and possibly profit - from reading about how we did it.

1

THE MAGNIFICENT VICTORY

You can lead a horse to water, but when you can get him to lie on his back and float, you've really got something.

- JOE E. LEWIS, *at the Cave Supper Club*, Vancouver

No doubt there are many ways of achieving heart-pounding excitement. Sky diving, bungee jumping, surfing a thunderous wave, and riding the up and down drafts in a hot air balloon over the Blue Ridge Mountains of Virginia come to mind.

For myself, though, there is absolutely nothing like the thrill of watching your underdog thoroughbred beat out a highly regarded champion by the proverbial nose in a big money race for claiming horses.

I'll never forget the memorable day it happened for me, a warm, sunny Saturday, July 20, 2003, at Canterbury Park in Shakopee, Minnesota.

Landler, a four-year-old chestnut gelding that one of our Hampshire partnerships had purchased for only $7,500, won the $48,000 National Claiming Crown "Express," becoming the year's 12th "winningest" horse in North America to that date and vaulting the Hampshire racing syndicate onto the front pages of the *Daily Racing Form* and the *Baltimore Sun*.

I went deliriously crazy along with trainer Dale Capuano, jockey Ryan Fogelsonger, a dozen syndicate partners and friends who had made the trip to Canterbury Park, and 16 other partners and pals who watched a simulcast at Laurel Park race track in Maryland. My only regret was that Hampshire co-founder Bill Joyce wasn't at Canterbury to share in the delirium. It was 15 years in the making.

The improbable win over Scott Lake's Pelican Beach, who at 3 to 5 odds was the overwhelming favorite of the six-race Claiming Crown card, boosted Landler's winnings over six months to almost $80,000, saving one of the two partnerships that owned him from bankruptcy.

Landler had defied every tipster and media analyst except the TVG Network commentator, who begged my Landler cap as a memento after the race, wearing it throughout the national telecast of the rest of the card. Pelican Beach was supposed to have had a "mortal lock" on the Claiming Crown "Express".

While Landler's win produced $26,400, anything less might have meant financial disaster for our budget-slim partnerships, since the roundtrip fare alone for our star performer was $11,000.

Dale Capuano admitted post-race that when we claimed Landler he could see some talent that needed to be developed but never in the trainer's wildest dreams did he believe Landler could rise to such heights.

Landler is walked in the paddock at Canterbury Park, MN,
prior to notching his 2003 Claiming Crown victory.

I personally had so much at stake (after all, I had approved the somewhat dicey $7,500 claim the previous January 30) I was much more inclined to think the Canadian-bred Landler had a shot, even at 9 to 2 odds.

Earlier, March 7, Landler had won his first race after we claimed him, an historic 100th victory for the Hampshire, by a significant 5 ¼ lengths at his home base, Laurel Park, winning $5,130, and on May 17 he had scored a Preakness Day win, the Maryland Heritage Purse worth $14,830, before 100,000 racing fans at Baltimore's historic Pimlico Race Course. Sandwiched between these two Hampshire milestones was a $12,000 victory at yet another race track, Delaware Park, on May 4.

Racing eight times that year, Landler was off the board only once, winning five times, taking second place twice. Contributing to that success: Capuano, Hampshire's longtime and talented trainer, had been for many years the top conditioner in Maryland. Also, the poster boy of Maryland tracks, jockey Ryan Fogelsonger was the current Eclipse Award winner, the industry's equivalent of Hollywood's Oscar, as the top apprentice in the nation.

So I stuck out my neck a few furlongs in a pre-race interview shown on Canterbury's Jumbotron. I bravely said: "We're optimistic that our horse can do it again."

I backed that up with a rare $50 wager, winning $285.

The Canterbury Park victory was the high point (so far) of a 14-year odyssey in the demanding, highly-competitive, and risk-riddled world of thoroughbred racing.

By that time Hampshire partnerships had placed almost 100 horses in 450 races at a wide range of racetracks. Besides Canterbury, they included Laurel Park, Pimlico and Timonium in Maryland, Colonial Downs in Virginia, Charles Town in West Virginia, Penn National and Philadelphia Park in Pennsylvania, Atlantic City and Meadowlands in New Jersey, Delaware Park, and Saratoga in New York.

Okay, we hadn't made a pile of money, but it was a lot more exciting than playing the stock market, and no one had taken a serious bath.

At this time in our existence, only two of our several dozen partnerships had ever gone bust; most other partnerships had returned between 25% and 105% to partners, and most described their experience as the best entertainment value for every dollar spent that they could imagine.

Not too shabby for a thoroughbred racing syndicate put together on a shoestring by an ex-journalist turned government bureaucrat and a lawyer in the Justice Department. To say that we were tyros is more than an understatement. More correctly, some said we were certifiable.

Thoroughbred racing is fraught with risk and is definitely not for the faint-hearted. Yet our gamble paid off and looking back now (and forward, too) I think I know the secret of our success. Work hard, learn from your mistakes, be innovative, never lose faith, share the risk (as well as the rewards), and keep smiling at every twist and turn along the way.

Upon reflection, that's probably a good recipe for any endeavor, but it strikes me as being particularly true of finding success in thoroughbred racing, and especially as to how we play the game in the Hampshire.

We've been able, over the years, to bring enjoyment and excitement - and, yes, sometimes disappointment and frustration - to the lives of more than 700 Hampshire investors, without making their ownership experience financially onerous and by providing a management service that gives them, forgive the cliché, the biggest bang for their bucks.

I know that few of our partners really expected to come out with a profit, although some of them did. Mostly, they were buying the entertainment value, and in that department it was worth every nickel spent.

Malcolm Barr, Sr., Hampshire president, receives the Maryland Heritage Purse trophy from State Secretary of Labor James D. Fielder, when Landler wins on the 2003 Preakness under card at Pimlico Race Course. (Photo by Jim McCue)

2
THE COCKTAIL
PARTY IDEA

Go anywhere in England where there are natural, wholesome, contented, and really nice English people; and what do you always find? That the stables are the real center of the household.

- BERNARD SHAW, *Heartbreak House*

In 1988, a couple of years after the tax act amendments had ravaged individual ownership in the thoroughbred industry, Bill Joyce and I happened to bump into each other at a cocktail party in Washington, D.C. We knew each other through working for the federal government.

Bill at this time was a Justice Department attorney with the Immigration and Naturalization Service. I also was at Justice, as director of public affairs at the Law Enforcement Assistance Administration. Conservative family men, though on opposite sides of the political spectrum, with homes in the capital's suburbs, we had, nevertheless, lost money in rather questionable racing ventures.

Bill had paid $5,000 for a horse named Indian Emperor who tended to lie down in his stall to sleep a few minutes before his race and usually left the gate last in the pack. He couldn't win a race at the county fair. Bill dropped several thousand dollars fooling around with him.

For my part, I had been in two limited partnerships, both destined from the outset to fail.

In the first, the trainer was the general partner and he had the family on the payroll. His son was the jockey, the girlfriend did the early gallops. Only the trainer won in this glowing example of conflict of interest. I also lost several thousand bucks.

In my other venture, the capitalization was far too low, and we went belly up in a few months. The fact that our $5,000 horse Nordic Conqueror scored two victories didn't make up for our $12,000 horse Grundoon being laid up the entire time with an ankle injury and never racing for us.

These losses were incurred before the tax law changes were enacted, so we fortunately were beneficiaries of those write-offs and depreciation allowances so necessary to give the industry a fighting chance. Back then some individual owners and limited partnerships stood to get up to 50 percent of their losses back via Uncle Sam.

Still, losing any amount of money foolishly is not pleasant, and Bill and I, as we talked at that cocktail party, got to wondering if - with the benefit of hindsight and experience - we couldn't make a success of limited partnerships.

Bill particularly had some definitive views. Chief was the need to spread ownership risk. The syndicate wouldn't own just one horse. It would own multiple horses. The more races we offered, the more satisfied our partners would be.

Also, we'd minimize overhead by doing all of the administrative work ourselves (with, as it turned out, a lot of help from our wives), and neither general partner would rely on the partnership for income.

Almost all funds raised would go directly into care and training of the horses. All charges to a partnership would be based on actual expenses.

Like excited kids with a new toy we gradually brought together a loose corporate entity. We called it a hobby. Friends raised eyebrows. "Uh, uh," they said, considering it yet another excuse for us to indulge a penchant for dabbling in the sport of kings.

As it turned out, it was neither hobby nor indulgence, but a lot of hard work. Setting up a new horse racing partnership involves a myriad of chores and we split them according to abilities and experience.

Bill stuck himself with the accounts and tax returns. I took on the marketing and communications (including a telephone hotline and newsletter). Recruiting the first partners and collecting their money was to be a joint effort. We also agreed to share the fun of enlisting a trainer and claiming our first horse. A friend, Richard Knight, was retained (pretty much pro bono) as the partnership lawyer.

Deciding on the syndicate's name and choosing its racing colors were two major time-consuming dramas. You may not realize it at the time but these are decisions you must live with for years hence.

Your name, and your racing colors, stay with you, even though the cast of characters - partnership clients, trainers, jockeys, horses - are subject to constant change. Look at it this way. *The New York Times* is stuck with being *The New York Times*. It can't change. Neither can the Hampshire. It has far too much invested in its name-recognition and reputation.

It took some doing but we finally got past the name and agreed on the Hampshire Racing Partnership. Bill's wife, Kathryn, had some pretty high falutin' ideas about life around the thoroughbreds, and Bill was on her side.

It was a choice they obviously had been harboring for a while. They had visions of the winner's circle at Churchill Downs the first Saturday in May. Or maybe it was the paddock under the trees in August in Saratoga (we finally got there!).

Me, I visualized a blue-collar partnership, but it was two against one and I went along, even agreeing to hard-to-read Old English lettering for the sake of adding a little class.

The name was never to be quite appropriate, though. It may have some degree of snob appeal, but, with very few exceptions, the Hampshire was never to attract snobs. Kathy, still trying to distance us from the hoi poloi, often wore her high-fashion, wide-brimmed sun hat in the winner's circle, but you'd find the rest of the gang in cutoffs and T-shirts.

Picking the syndicate's colors also threatened to get out of hand before Bill and I wisely decided to withdraw, leaving it to Kathy (we were too busy with other matters, we claimed). My wife, Carol, skeptical of the enterprise, had declined an initial invitation to participate, so she didn't have any say.

Ironically, Kathy came up with Carol's favorite color, pink. To be precise, hot pink and black diamonds, black bands with pink stripes on the sleeves, and pink cuffs. So that was settled without high drama. But we had only just started.

Now we had to recruit our initial partners, collect their money, form the first partnership, get permission to race, find a trainer, buy (or claim) a horse, pick a jockey, and on and on.

"Whoa," Bill said. "What have we gotten into?"

"Hey," I reminded him. "It's only a hobby."

"Don't keep saying that," he cautioned. "We've got ourselves a business."

"OK, already. It's only a small business…why is it a business?"

"The IRS…" he said, darkly.

First on our shopping list was a trainer. Based on past experience, we were convinced that having a top trainer would be the key to the success of both the initial partnership and the syndicate's ongoing operations.

At the time, in the late 1980s, there were perhaps two trainers in Maryland worth considering. One, King Leatherbury, had for many years led the state, and sometimes the nation, in races won. The King still ruled but hot on his heels was a relative youngster from a Pennsylvania horse family named Dale Capuano.

Capuano, then aged 25, had already won his first state racing title and was putting it to the much larger Leatherbury stable, despite having about one fifth the number of horses. We did the arithmetic. Capuano had about 40 horses. Leatherbury had 240, or thereabouts. From that perspective, if Capuano was crowding Leatherbury, then he had to be the best, right? So we chose to go with the young man who had a reputation as a "hands on" trainer with an "almost magical touch" with race horses.

Next problem, getting an introduction. In those days, most trainers were fat and happy, some disdainful of a partnership's business. They didn't want the hassle of a dozen owners of one horse. We needed an "in".

Happily, we got it from one of my friends, Larry Lacey, who I happened to bump into in the $2 bettors' line one Saturday afternoon at Laurel race track.

I quietly confided in him about our plans and he whispered Capuano's name behind his hand (guys are always whispering behind their hands in bettors' lines). "He's a kid with a future," Lacey said, conspiratorially.

I told him I already knew that. The problem was, how to arrange a meeting? Would he put us together?

Not a problem. Capuano was Lacey's ex-wife's cousin, and, even several times removed, that carried weight in the tightly knit Capuano family.

I accepted this with high hopes, as Lacey was a very likeable guy, unlikely to be drummed out of the tribe on account of a little thing like a divorce . When, as a teen-ager, he briefly fell in love with first wife, then twice his age, I couldn't get angry with him. Lilia was admittedly quite a looker and what's wrong with a young man willing to run errands and do odd jobs when the only reward is a smile?

Anyway, Lacey went to bat for me, the meeting was arranged, and Capuano said any friend of Larry was a friend of his. Yes, he would claim horses for us, and yes, he would board, train and race them for us.

Very personable and obliging, Larry was to die of a heart attack a few weeks later, shy of his fortieth birthday. I'm glad he stuck around long enough to get us off on the right foot and that's why this book is dedicated to him.

3

THE FIRST PARTNERSHIP

One never rises so high as when one does not know where one is going.

- OLIVER CROMWELL, *Remark,* to M. Bellievre

Okay. Off to the races. We had our assigned responsibilities, we had our syndicate's name, we had our colors, we had our trainer, and we had a long and very impressive legal contract to present to would-be partners.

Just one thing was missing. The partners.

Bill and I felt like neophyte life insurance salesmen as we phoned around to friends, relatives and business acquaintances, asking if they were interested in buying a $1,000 share in the Hampshire. Most of them wrote us off as being slightly weird.

Not to be dissuaded, we took out a small but costly advertisement in the *Daily Racing Form* and sat back and waited. And waited. And waited. Nothing happened.

Whereupon we learned the answer to the riddle of which came first, the chicken or the egg. It was the egg.

We had the best trainer in the state, we had the sharpest colors, we had that impressive legal document, but we didn't have a track record.

To get a track record, we needed a horse. To get a horse, we needed money. To get money, we needed partners. (The egg is in there somewhere. You decide. In any event, it is not the chicken.)

Taking stock, we bought another ad in the *Daily Racing Form*, and this time we installed our "hotline," so if you responded to the ad you'd get a recorded, if not a personal, sales pitch. We also printed up business cards with that telephone number and handed them out almost indiscriminately. And we talked to anyone who would listen.

My wife wants me to say we talked ourselves hoarse. I refuse. Anyway, the hotline was to become the underpinning of our little hobby/business.

Eventually, in November, 1988, six months after the cocktail party that gave birth to the syndicate idea, we had recruited a dozen partners and achieved our goal of a $25,000 capitalization. Half of the money came from those aforementioned friends, relatives and business acquaintances, with some purchasing more than one share. Bill and I bought one share each to close the offering.

The cost of raising the money, putting the legal papers together, becoming licensed as owners, and attending to the other myriad details was less than $1,000.

We hotfooted it out to the barn at the Bowie Training Center in Bowie, Maryland, with a $14,000 check, expecting to sign a contract with our trainer, Dale Capuano, only to learn it doesn't work that way. In the nether world of thoroughbred racing a signed document is about as rare as a diesel truck that doesn't spew pollution.

Capuano told us to put the $14,000 in the horsemen's account at the track, make sure that he had power of attorney (describing him as our "authorized agent" and permitting him to do virtually whatever he liked with the money), and then he would let us know when he had a claim in mind.

We looked at the chart of horses on the grimy desk in the down-at-the-heels cubicle that served as the office of Maryland's most successful trainer. Capuano seemed younger than remembered at that moment. He also was perhaps more taciturn.

Bill and I exchanged glances, shrugged haplessly, figured we had no option but to trust him, said good-bye and left.

At the track, we used our new white plastic "badges" to gain admittance, then sauntered into the racing secretary's office, feigning nonchalance. In truth, we were sweating.

This was a new world, and we were out-of-place, uncomfortable, and frankly a little suspicious. Everyone in the smoky office (this was 1989, remember), most of whom were trainers and grooms, seemed to be looking at us appraisingly. It wasn't the normal playing field for a federal attorney and a government public relations guy.

Tentatively, we handed our $14,000 check to the cashier. She looked us over, made a book entry, and slid the check into a drawer, telling us it would be good in 10 days.

Ten days! It seemed like it would be forever before Capuano could claim the first horse for the Hampshire Racing Partnership.

Actually, it was almost a month, December 8, 1988, before Capuano suggested we claim a nondescript four-year-old chestnut gelding named Duke Toby. We got the Duke for $6,500 and when we reported the purchase at our first shareholders meeting that month you would have thought we had claimed a Secretariat.

We had, in fact, paid top dollar for the Duke, since for nine races he had worn a $5,000 claiming tag. However, he had won the last two of those races, and his overall lifetime record wasn't too shabby. He had won five, placed twice, posted four shows.

The first meeting of Hampshire I's 14 syndicate members, ranging from lawyers to bellhops to a retired CEO, was held at the National Press Club in Washington, D.C. I'm a member by virtue of my background in journalism and I'm always glad to take advantage of the certain cachet the club enjoys in Washington. The president is a member, as have been all his modern-day predecessors at the White House, and it is the soapbox for heads of state around the world.

Amid loud applause, exuberant backslapping and boundless speculation, we ended our first meeting with a promise to get together again at the races, whether it be weekday or weekend, workday or day off.

It was a particularly bad winter and we were snowed out three times before we finally got the Duke to the races on January 17, 1989. He didn't disappoint us, though. He flashed first past the winning post and treated us all to our first big rush as thoroughbred owners. He did it again later that month to make it two straight with a young apprentice jockey, Kent Desormeaux. He was claimed from us after the second victory on January 28, leaving $9,600 in purse money behind.

Not to be outdone, Super Operator, the partnership's second claim on February 6, at $5,000, also scored two first-place victories in a row. That made it four consecutive victories in four weeks, first with the kid, Desormeaux, in the irons, then with Mario Pino riding. This time $13,000 in earnings. Easy!

I was denied the pleasure of witnessing the Duke's second win because I was 6,000 miles away in Hawaii on a previously planned vacation to the islands I'd worked and lived in during the l960s. I would have much preferred to be in Maryland on that cold January day than lollygagging on a sunny beach in Waikiki. That's what thoroughbred racing can do to your head even when you own but a fraction of a beat-up bangtail.

Smarting from the experience, I was to miss only one of the syndicate's next 30 races, and then only because we had two horses scheduled to run on the same day at different tracks. Bill had opted for Beach Ballerina, our first two-year-old purchase, competing at Pimlico, so I drove my family 150 miles to watch Due It Smoothly at Penn National. Beach Ballerina won. Smoothly came in fifth.

With the perversity one only sees in horse racing, the next time out, stepping up in class, Smoothly won with ease - in our absence.

The Duke's two straight wins saw him pay for himself in six weeks of ownership. The Operator, claimed at a lower price, but run at a much higher classification, managed to give us a profit, but only briefly.

After our first quarter, the expenses we racked up in the process - about $40 a day each to board and train the horses, plus hefty vet bills - ate away at our capital.

We were winning races, but we were already losing money! We obviously had a tough row to hoe if the syndicate was going to keep partners happy and achieve lasting success. It was a manifestation of things to come. The claiming game can be exciting, but it's tough to stay ahead financially.

Meanwhile, individually, as loyal, that's-my-horse bettors, most of us were making money at the windows. It didn't matter that you owned a relatively small share. It was "your" horse and you were inclined to wager heavily. My own personal return from the betting windows shot up like never before.

Prompted by our early success, some partners continued to bet heavily, but most, like myself, are more prudent now. A jump start at the races can be as dangerous as an early coup on the stock market.

I'll never forget the warning I received from my boss in the Department of Commerce. Secretary Malcolm Baldrige, when he heard of the killing I'd made on American Express, said, "You'll be sorry ... "

Two years later, I had lost the AmEx profits and more besides, prompting my return to horse racing. At least I find pleasure in seeing the ponies compete. I'd rather watch a traffic jam than glean the stock pages.

When we set out, shares cost $1,000, then $1,500, then $2,500, with a capitalization per partnership of $20,000 to $25,000. Through the years, we've increased this slightly, and the claiming partnerships in 2005 were running $2,500 to $3,500 to get in, with the capitalization usually $35,000. In later partnerships where we purchased young, un-raced horses off the farm, the capitalization can run as high as high as $75,000.

If a partnership doesn't proceed, all money is refunded. If it goes ahead, we try to dissolve it in two to three years, with funds divided based on a partner's percentage stake.

As general partners in our earlier partnerships, Bill and I participated in this win/lose settlement, as we always took a minor cash position in every partnership, signaling our confidence in the concept.

I have always tried to be as frugal as possible in managing the Hampshire. At first, Bill and I each took only 5 % of purses for our trouble, as well as just 5 % of any profit from the sale of horses, either through claims or by private sale. Later, as running partnerships became more time-consuming - preparing Schedule Ks for 30 people at income tax time during the limited partnership days, for instance - we charged a 2 % management fee off the top. It didn't begin to cover the hours spent, but it's a hobby, remember. Not really.

The care and training of the horses, borne by the individual partnerships, accounted then, as now, for 85 % or so of our costs. Incidental expenses, such as those for phone bills, stationery and stamps, are shared between the various partnerships. Sharing keeps the overhead quite low.

For the usual legal and tax reasons, the Hampshire incorporated in 1996. I became president, Bill vice president, Kathy secretary, and Carol treasurer. Shortly thereafter, Bill and Kathy left for Massachussets, where Bill became a federal immigration judge. He has since retired from the bench and is in private practice in Boston.

Bill took his Hampshire duties with him to Boston, but it became impractical for him to keep up with the horses, the trainers and veterinarians from there, so Carol became our bookkeeper, a job she has held ever since, and I ran the various racing and breeding partnerships.

Carol had spent most of her career with the federal government, much of that time handling budgets amounting to millions of dollars for the U.S. Customs Service in Washington, and that made transition relatively easy, but by no means a cakewalk. From the mid-1990s, the Hampshire moved from just two partnerships with a couple of dozen participants, to nine partnerships with almost 80 investors.

"It became really time-consuming and difficult to keep everything separate, since even with the corporate umbrella, we treated each group separately," Carol recalls.

"Each group had to stand on its own, as, well, a partnership. To identify them, we began to name them after famous racetracks such as Epsom, Santa Anita, Woodbine, Saratoga, and so on."

Most years, Carol has brought the administrative overhead of these partnerships down to an average of 5%, sometimes permitting as much as 95% of our funds to go to the purchase, care and training of our animals.

As the official treasurer, Carol is the corporation's only salaried employee, receiving $50 a month per partnership - but only when it's making money!

At an annual meeting a few years ago Carol was voted a $50 bonus from every winner's purse. So, for example, when Lunar Indian won a $16,000 purse, Carol smiled all the way to the bank with an extra $50. Frugality runs both ways at the Hampshire.

When Bill gave up the books, I altered the 10% commission on purses that we had shared, reducing the take to 7 ½ % of purses. I also dropped the management fee except in the case of breeding partnerships, which are charged $450 a year. In a breeding partnership, no income is generated for the first several years, but they still must be serviced.

Using the Hampshire Alliance as an umbrella for several partnerships that are treated quite separately as individual groups, it is sometimes difficult to get our business associates, such as trainers, breeders, van companies, vets, etc., to understand this when they see us pick up a big check for one horse, then plead an extra few days to pay their bill, which would be on behalf of a horse owned by another group.

We cannot borrow money from a prospering partnership to prop up one that is lagging, so, in essence, they are still "partnerships" and not mini corporations. Complicated, but it works.

Bill Joyce in Boston continues as vice-president of the Hampshire and prepares and submits our tax returns to the IRS. He's our in-house legal guru and our point man in times of trial and trouble, all pretty much pro bono.

CLAIMING

The first favourite was never heard of, the second favourite was never seen after the distance post, all the ten-to-oners were in the rear, and a dark horse, which had never been thought of ... rushed past the grand stand to sweeping triumph.

- BENJAMIN DISRAELI, *The Young Duke*

In the claiming business, finding good horses at a reasonable price is like looking for the mushrooms in mushroom soup. It's slim pickings. You also need the breaks, and our best break, as it turned out, was a break in the weather.

January through March, 2003, was one of the worst winters on record in Maryland racing, with Laurel Park shut down, off and on, ice and snow, for five weeks.

January 30, a rare sunny and pleasant day, drew Dale Capuano and me to Laurel, and that's when Capuano spotted Landler, who was to score that magnificent upset win at Canterbury Park.

Capuano was impressed both by Landler's pedigree as well as the claiming tag of $7,500.

I agreed that Landler was well bred, having a champion Canadian sire, Langfuhr, the dam Delightful, by Bold Ruckus. However, he had a ho-hum record, one win and one second place in 14 starts.

"He's worth a shot," Capuano insisted, and since he was the expert, I went along, agreeing to the $7,500 claim.

Landler, incidentally, was but one of 120 horses we were to claim between 1988 and 2005, spending an estimated $850,000.

For the uninitiated, claiming a horse simply means a licensed owner or trainer buying a horse at a pre-determined price set by a track's racing secretary before the race takes place. Horses of the most limited ability may appear in a program with $5,000 claiming tags and for intermediate horses it may range from $15,000 to $30,000.

Few races are carded for high-priced claimers where we normally race our horses (Maryland, Virginia, West Virginia, Pennsylvania, New Jersey, Delaware) but there are claimers that can be purchased for $40,000 to $75,000. A recent Kentucky Derby winner, Charismatic, once competed in a $65,000 claiming race!

Claiming races comprise perhaps 80% of racing programs throughout the United States. Claiming tends to keep the game honest. When you enter a horse with a claiming tag, horses of a similar caliber will race against it. For example, you would not enter a superior horse in a $5,000 claiming race. It would win, yes. But it would be claimed. You may lose a horse worth $20,000 to win a $6,000 purse share. Not smart.

If you want to claim a horse, you drop a claim in a box in the racing secretary's office. The horse becomes yours after the race, no matter the outcome. You may end up with a winner or loser or be so unfortunate as to have claimed a horse that was injured and never finished the race. It has happened to us.

Managing claiming partnerships is relatively simple in that it is possible to fairly accurately project the cost of the horse plus the cost of getting them into the races based on the daily training stipend, the average vet bills, plus the minor administration costs incurred by the partnerships . Assuming a capitalization of $30,000, you claim just one horse at a time, and you claim low, if you can. Our magic number is $8,500, which, including tax, represents a $9,000 capital expenditure.

A claiming horse should be back to racing for the partnerships within a month of entering his new stable. Training costs, plus vet bills, for that month, are estimated at $2,000 to $2,200.

We figure our trainer can improve the horse, run him at the $12,000 claiming level the first time out, and perhaps win 60% of a $15,000 purse .

If so, we are in a position to claim a second horse almost immediately. If he merely places or shows, or runs out of the money, then we wait, run him back down at $8,500 or less, his next race dictating whether we claim another, or, again, wait.

If he is claimed away from us without winning a purse, then we can still go ahead and claim another, probably at the same price.

When we are fortunate enough to win, we can increase the claiming parameters, say to a high of $12,500 or even $15,000.

Should the amount of money in the pot get down to less than $10,000, we disband the partnership and distribute the remaining money among the partners, as there isn't sufficient money to claim a horse *and* support him.

Otherwise, we normally operate a partnership for two years and share any remaining money based on share ownership at the end of that period and after all horses have been disposed of. We give the partnership management up to a year to do this to avoid any fire sale of good horses.

To date, we have returned 25% to 130% on all but one claiming partnership. That partnership went totally broke!

After we acquired Landler, he went to his new home at Capuano's stables at Laurel and the cost of keeping him soon threatened to catch up to the cost of buying him. Due to the bad weather, Landler and his Hampshire stable mates, Pick Me Buzz and Dronero, were unable to race all of February and most of March.

Together the three shut-ins were racking up training fees and vet bills of about $180 a day - and no income.

When Landler finally got to the track, winning that historic 100th victory for us with Ryan Fogelsonger aboard March 7 at Laurel, the $5,130 purse wasn't enough to keep the wolf from the door. Sometime, and soon, something had to be done, as this was an impending crisis.

Our answer was to split Landler into two ownership groups, with the Maryland partnership that owned him selling 50% of his value, then upped to $15,000, to a sister partnership in West Virginia. The latter had plenty of money but no horses.

We had adopted this unique horse-sharing scheme once before after a debacle with a horse named Foolish World (and more about him later) had provoked us into some creative thinking.

Extending Landler's ownership from the original 10 partners to a total of 26 also meant there were a lot more investors to enjoy the fun that was to come, but when the money from purses started rolling in, we did hear some gripes.

On May 4, when Landler scored another impressive victory, winning by 4½ lengths at Delaware Park under jockey Rodrigo Madrigal, Jr., the purse put $6,000 into each of the two partnership accounts. A couple of members of the original group that owned all of Landler noted that without the split they'd have gotten $12,000. They apparently forgot that Landler, without even money enough for van fare, would have stayed home, meaning they'd have gotten a fat zero.

Landler's 6-furlong, 1 minute, 11 2/5th seconds win at Delaware Park was sufficiently impressive for him to earn his way onto the undercard on Preakness Day, the second leg of the Triple Crown, which attracted a crowd of 120,000 to historic Pimlico Race Course at Baltimore on May 17.

This was a trophy race, a $35,000, 6-furlong allowance sprint for the Maryland Heritage Purse, and it marked the Hampshire's first time in a Triple Crown program.

Once more, with Fogelsonger back in the irons, Landler won, surging past our deliriously screaming group in mid-stretch to a two-length victory worth $14,830. I frankly was almost at a loss for words - very unusual, as my wife and many others will attest - when James D. Fielder, Jr., the state's secretary of labor, presented the trophy to me.

In his next outing, June 28 at Colonial Downs, one of the nation's newest and loveliest race courses, a few miles outside historic Williamsburg, Landler got to the winner's circle yet again. With Fogelsonger aboard, he won a starter allowance by half a length while scoring a 6-furlong career best, 1minute, 9 seconds flat.

The Colonial Downs race was the last test to determine whether Landler should be entered in the National Claiming Crown competition at Canterbury.

Now we had to wait to see if he made the cut, judged by total purse money.

By this time, Landler had produced $49,275 in purses, winning four of his six races and placing second in the two others. Our $7,500 bargain was starting to be compared to

Funny Cide, the so-called "cheap" horse owned by the upstate New York syndicate, Sackatoga Stable, who won the Derby and the Preakness but failed at Belmont Park. Coincidentally, the following year, Landler's sire, Langfuhr, was inducted into the Canadian Horse Racing Hall of Fame.

Years earlier, Capuano was right on the money when we bought Probably The One, a lightly run five-year-old mare, from a $6,500 claiming race July 30, 1990, at Laurel.

She had been raced only seven times, winning about $7,000, and this was her second time out in two years, indicating a possible injury. Still, Capuano liked the look of her, and oh, boy, was that a good call. Overall, she didn't win us as much money as Landler, but she had more going for her than simply being a fast filly.

She quickly became the darling of our partners, playing Jekyll and Hyde. The heart of the lioness that she showed on the track was coupled with a gentle disposition in the stall. Her antics amused and delighted everyone - especially the kids.

For a while, racing in Maryland, she was the fastest older female in her class over six furlongs, and we soon had her at the $35,000 claiming and $21,000 allowance levels.

When, due to arthritis, we were forced to retire her, Probably The One had squeaked through to join the illustrious ranks of horses that win more than $100,000 in a lifetime.

Her record:

Races	Win	Place	Show	Earnings
31	10	9	3	$100,756

With several fourth-place finishes to her credit, she was rarely off the board.

As I've said, most of our partners were essentially blue-collar types, but we did have the one millionaire, Bill Verity, the former Secretary of Commerce who, before joining us, had won a $50 wager on Duke Toby. Verity and his wife, Peggy, had owned high-end thoroughbreds, but they'd never had a winner. Now, even though they owned just a small share of a cheap claiming horse, they were delighted to have a champion in Probably The One, and they were anxious to watch her perform.

The chance came on a chilly day in January, 1991, when Verity had a meeting on Capitol Hill, and Probably The One was in a $16,000 claiming race at Laurel. The Veritys drove down to catch it.

In the paddock, Probably The One was in fine fettle, mugging for the cameras and generally making herself agreeable for Peggy and Bill, but Capuano's sister, Gina, was dismayed. Didn't we know that taking a picture of your horse before a race was bad luck?

Oh, no! The Veritys and I went to our box thinking that was just a silly superstition, but what if … ?

Jockey Donald Miller and trainer Dale Capuano (right) with former U.S. Commerce Secretary Bill Verity and wife Peggy at the Laurel Park paddock in 1991. Bill Verity was an early member of the Hampshire partnerships.

We really sweated the race. Running just off the pace, it looked like Probably The One wouldn't win, and then she provided us with her usual nail-biting finish, flashing to the front just before the wire and winning by half a length.

Probably The One's owners had their picture taken in the winner's circle (no superstitions about that) and the Veritys hung a handsomely framed memento in the lobby of their fine waterfront home in South Carolina's historic Beaufort.

Rich or poor, when you have your picture taken in the winner's circle, the photograph can be as important as the money, probably more so.

Dr. Martha Riche, former director of the U.S. Census Bureau, was another of our "big name" partners, but she never bet on a horse, preferring to visit them and watch the races.

Our joyride with Probably The One ended when bone chips that required expensive surgery were discovered in her left knee. Normally, Bill Joyce and I ran the syndicate dictatorially, but in this instance, because of the expense, and the fact that she'd be off at least six months, we asked the partners to approve the operation.

They did, and almost a year to the day after she was claimed, Probably The One was sent to a top-rated veterinary surgeon at the University of Pennsylvania at New Bolton. The operation was a success but the prognosis was gloomy. The vet said the arthritis he came across would make it difficult for us to race her in the future.

We tried anyway, nursing her back to reasonably good health on the farm, and when we felt she was ready, entered her in a $12,000 claiming race at Laurel in January, 1992. It was one of the bleakest, rainiest days of the winter, but our plucky mare still managed to finish first, winning $4,800 as her share of the purse. It was that win that carried her to the lifetime record above $100,000.

Sadly, she came out of the race sore, and when she ran again three weeks later, in a $6,500 claiming race, she finished a poor fifth.

It was decision time. In two more weeks she was to be entered at the $5,000 claiming level. If claimed, that would boost her overall earnings for us, but there was an equal chance of her breaking down.

We polled the partners, who elected to retire her -and breed her.

Based on emotion, that was a bad, long-shot business decision. Apart from her, Probably The One's parents hadn't produced much by the way of successful racing offspring.

But try telling that to the partners. Probably The One had never let us down before. They were sure she wouldn't disappoint us as a mother. Besides, and Bill and I concurred in this, wholeheartedly, we owed her a big debt.

The next chapter tells you what happened.

5
BREEDING

*Men are generally more careful of the breed of their horses
and dogs than of their children.*

- WILLIAM PENN, *Some Fruits of Solitude*

I've found over the years that claiming thoroughbreds and
breeding them are as different as picking daisies and running
a marathon.

When you claim a horse, like picking a daisy, you are in
business right away, able to race him every two weeks or so.

An equine pregnancy spans 11 months. And then the
newborn, God willing, is still at least two years away from its
first race. That's a long, long haul.

With our first try, Probably The One, we did get off to a fast
start, though. Within 24 hours of putting together a $7,500
verbal partnership proposal, the Hampshire had commitments,
or cash in hand, to breed her. Ten partners had bought in for
$750 each to share in the first year's expenses.

In February, 1992, we established her at Wyemore Farm in rural Church Hill, Maryland, in the care of Dale Capuano's uncle, Louis, and his wife, Christine.

Then I had a fateful talk with Capuano's father, Philip, meeting with the noted horseman in a dingy coffee shop at the now-shuttered Bowie Race Track, an adjunct shed row for trainers not fortunate enough to get stalls at nearby Laurel.

Phil was a tall, thick-set, silver-haired man nearing 60, my age at the time, so we had a natural rapport in the hour-long conversation that passed for my early education in equine breeding.

He allowed that our mare Probably The One had "some speed" in her pedigree (Exclusive One-Fortune Fleur by Swoon's Son) and that his stallion Private Key brought "stamina" from his distinguished parents, Private Account and Key to the Mint. An expensive horse, Private Key had been injured early in training, had never gotten into competition, and was waiting, still untested, in a breeding shed at Edmar Farm in Frederick, Maryland.

It wasn't exactly a match made in heaven but worth experimenting with and the price was right - zero dollars. That left our $7,500 intact to maintain Probably The One through her pregnancy.

In March, Louis and Christine dutifully prepped her, a complicated procedure "under the lights" to help her cycle into estrus, and then off she went to Edmar Farm, for her date with destiny.

Private Key was given a couple of shots at our lovely brood mare, just to make sure, as we had been told that first-time mares, especially those arriving at a breeding shed directly from a racetrack, could be problematical. She made it with one or the other and the countdown began.

Probably The One spent that summer grazing with a small band of mares in the fields of Wymore Farm. Church Hill is between Annapolis and Wilmington, Delaware, so for most partners, living in and around Washington, it was a two-hour drive to pay "Momma" a visit.

Fortunately, that could be combined with a trip to the track, and it was a great spot to take the kids, who came stocked with treats. Probably The One would invariably separate herself from her pals and come over for apples and carrots and peppermint candy. It was always an emotional moment for me to watch her gently take something from my young son's hand, and I invariably choked up a bit when it was time to leave.

Part of that came from knowing she was among the small percentage of thoroughbreds who get any sort of life when their racetrack days are over. In those days, most went to the knacker yard for slaughter and this is the dark side of racing. Fortunately, a number of farms - Summerwind Farm in Libertytown, Maryland, comes to mind - are springing up that care for injured or worn-out racehorses, and hopefully that trend will continue.

We didn't get out to see Probably The One as often during the winter, but she continued to do well, and in February, at the height of the worst snow storm in years, she gave birth to a healthy boy, although it was touch and go for a while.

Murphy, as the farm hands came to call him, before he got a proper monicker, had a lot of trouble feeding. Veterinarian Mary Tubman complained, "I'll give this mare 100 percent for personality but zero percent for nipples!"

To make sure the newborn got enough milk, Louis spent the first two days in the stall 'round the clock, holding him up to his mom's diminutive teats every two hours.

"He got stronger and stronger, and on the third day, when he tried to kick me, that's when I figured he had turned the corner," Louis said. "That's when I knew I could get out of there and get some sleep."

The breeding partnership group had been ready with champagne and cigars but the blizzard conditions denied any of us from being there for the big event. Mark Hytowitz and Laurie Hamilton, used to tough weather in Philadelphia, were the first partners on the scene, arriving within six hours after the birth.

They provided the rest of the group with the first on-site reports from the barn, as well as the first pictures. Bill Joyce's wife, Kathryn, got there not long after, so there was ample maternal concern.

At two weeks, when the weather had changed from freezing cold and snow to brilliant, if still cold, sunshine, more of us gathered to watch "Momma" lead her baby out to the pasture for the first time. As they gamboled in the fresh, bracing winter air, it was a day of joy and a true high point for the Hampshire.

Coincidentally, it was that weekend that Sir Beaufort, one of the colt's relatives on his father's side, won the Santa Anita Derby.

Probably The One with her first-born, Key Probability, known to all as "Murphy."

Six months later, we held a picnic meeting at the paddock, watching our gangly "teen-ager" frolic in the summer sunshine. Partner Richard Popkin, Washington attorney, proposed the name we all voted on - Key Probability. To the farm hands he was still Murphy, a name they had bestowed earlier, around the time, when he was three months old, that he suffered a grievous injury to his left eye. He was left blind in that eye for the rest of his life, but was a useful racehorse nevertheless, adapting to his handicap as his doctor said he would.

The last time I saw him was at Penn National, where he was claimed for $5,000. During his two-year racing career with the Hampshire, he raced 17 times, won just once, was second three times, and third three times. Because of that blind eye, the grooms there called him Sammy Davis, Jr., but for most of the time we owned him, five years in all, he remained Murphy to us

Bill and Kathy Joyce adopted a farm puppy around that time and called him Murphy too. The dog, a nervous black mutt, was still living with the Joyces in Duxbury, MA, as we were finishing writing this book in 2005.

I regret not knowing what happened to Murphy the horse. In those days, in the early 1990s, we were not as given to looking out for our horses as we are today. Today, we endeavor, as best we can, to find homes for them when their racing days are over.

Encouraged by their success, Probably The One's partners decided to try breeding her again, this time to a proven sire, Corridor Key, whose father, Danzig, was a U.S. "sire of sires" in 1992. The handsome gray stallion was producing stakes-winning progeny at the state's oldest and perhaps most respected breeding establishment, Country Life Farm in Bel Air, Maryland, at a price we could afford - $2,000.

Probably The One and her foal were vanned to Bel Air and once again she had little trouble conceiving. She experienced an uneventful pregnancy and gave birth to a second colt, nicknamed Opie, who was eventually named, again on a vote of partners, Hampshire Lad.

So now we had two offspring of our former $6,500 claimer. Louis and Christine Capuano had moved to a bigger farm nearby, Circle C Training Center, where both healthy foals, one now a yearling, the other just a gangly baby, and their mom, she of the inverted nipples, lived. Getting enough milk was never easy for Momma's kids.

For a third sire, we settled on Hay Halo, a 10-year-old former Maryland Juvenile Champion (1986), who was standing at Green Willow Farms in Westminster, Maryland. We paid a $1,500 stud fee.

Again, Probably The One conceived readily, and once more gave birth without a problem, this time giving us her first filly, Probably's Halo.

Tragically, while the foal was being born, Hampshire Lad-- Opie--was fighting for his life at New Bolton Veterinary Center in Pennsylvania, the victim of a raging bacterial infection. Just 48 hours later, two days before his first birthday, Opie was euthanized.

Altogether, Louis and Christine Capuano helped Probably The One birth five foals for us, and the four who survived - Key Probability, Probably's Devil, Hampshire Dancer and Probably's Halo - were all winners. They not only got to the races, but all made it to the winner's enclosure.

Hampshire Dancer was our first stakes horse, though not winning at that level, and Probably's Devil took us to the famed Saratoga race track in upstate New York. He didn't win there either, but gave us an experience in big-time racing to remember forever. The Devil found a permanent home in retirement, but Hampshire Dancer, we later learned, was rescued virtually from the doors of the abattoir by a caring family, but died shortly thereafter. Her owners asked for a winner's circle photograph as a memento, which we sent.

Even though they have children of their own, Louis and Christine were another pair who treated horses like kids, doing everything humanly possible on their behalf. They tended to struggle more than other members of the extended Capuano family and could never quite hit one out of the park with a consistent major contender.

While breeding for us, Louis was kicked in the sternum by a horse - not one of ours, thankfully - and had to be air evacuated to hospital in Baltimore. He pulled through, but almost died.

I trust it is atypical of the business that one Hampshire partner didn't appreciate Louis being off the job for so long. Mister Sympathetic was overheard asking what Louis thought he was doing standing behind a horse anyway.

Oskaloosa, another of our mares, also was to provide us with a winning homebred, but her breeding partnership was stalked by tragedy.

I decided to breed Oskaloosa after she suffered a severely injured ankle and could not race. This was a couple of years before my 70th birthday, and Carol, aware of the long-term commitment that breeding entailed, wondered if I planned to be racing her offspring when I turned 80.

The reminder of my mortality didn't deter me, however. By this time I was a dedicated horseman. I could always cheer on her progeny from a gurney and while in diapers.

So I floated another 10-member partnership, $750 each, and called in a chit that Josh Pons of Country Life Farm had given me after Probably The One lost Hampshire Lad from the breeding with Corridor Key.

Pons offered us an affordable date with his promising new stallion, Malibu Moon, a son of Kentucky Derby winner A.P. Indy.

In a league of her own with young horses, Susan Runco, the wife of trainer Jeff Runco, was serving as our advisor at the time, and she was instrumental in helping us decide on Pons' untried Malibu Moon to cover Oskaloosa, a descendent of a decent stallion named Waquoit.

Susan explained all the reasons why the cross, which included Mr. Prospector, a U.S. sire of sires, was a natural that could pay big dividends. She told us, "You could be looking at a match made in heaven!"

Born in April, 2002, Lunar Indian, Oskaloosa's foal by Malibu Moon, grew to be so big (17-plus hands) that he was well past three years old before he was sufficiently developed where we could think of racing him. Given that his illustrious father had risen from a $5,000 sire in Maryland to a $30,000 stud in Kentucky, and had strewn a score of high-class stakes progeny, including Declan Moon, around the country and the world, the expectations of his group of 10 owners were by the fall of 2005 running pretty high.

To take advantage of the high purse structure in West Virginia, we had foaled Lunar Indian's mom, Oskaloosa, in that state at O'Sullivan Farm, although the breeding had taken place at Country Life in Maryland. Trainer Dale Capuano therefore chose a Maiden Special 6 1/2 furlong open race in October, 2005, at Charles Town for Lunar Indian to make his debut. All 10 partners were there, including Chuck Montgomery, 77, who drove a 400-mile round trip from Virginia Beach with his wife Dorothy.

Ridden by veteran Charles Town jockey Anthony Mawing, Lunar Indian, a brown colt with a huge white blaze, seemed more interested in the crowd and the overhead lights - Charles

Town races mostly at night - than on racing, and it took Anthony all his wiles and strength to keep the horse's attention on his job. He didn't win, but he ran second, and showed enough ability to tell us that perhaps, just perhaps, he had enough of his father in him to give us an outstanding race horse in the future. We were excited about our prospect.

After the race, Mawing told the trainer, "Put blinkers on him next time and we've got ourselves a winner!"

That's exactly what Capuano did, and that's exactly what happened. Against a field of state-bred horses, this time at 7 furlongs, Lunar Indian went wire to wire, winning by three lengths and enriching the partnership by more than $30,000 by his two races, including owners and breeders bonuses that came with racing on his home turf.

Hampshire president Malcolm Barr, Sr. with proud mom, Oskaloosa, and first son, Lunar Indian, by Malibu Moon.

We thought that Lunar Indian's successes would compensate for the heartache that had plagued Oskaloosa's other offspring, but it was not to be. He was to be laid up for the best part of 2006 with serious problems with his suspensory ligaments.

In July, 2003, Oskaloosa's next foal following Lunar Indian, already named Hampshire Court, died at seven weeks after a brief bout with pneumonia. The death occurred just four days after he had been visited, seemingly in good health, by some 60 partners and guests at a Hampshire picnic at O'Sullivan Farm.

As Hampshire Court struggled for life in Morven Park animal hospital in Leesburg, Virginia, several of his owners were at Canterbury Park in Minnesota, to watch Landler, owned by two other Hampshire partnership groups, race for the National Claiming Crown.

They heard of the death only hours before the race . Some wept openly before the tears were swept away by Landler's victory. It is the kind of two-sided sword one often encounters in thoroughbred racing.

The following year, Oskaloosa's third foal, by the stallion Makin, took sick with septicemia which attacked his stifles (hips). We put him in a nearby equine hospital, REACH, before moving him to Marie Draus's Stonewall Farm in Virginia. There, in 'round the clock shifts, we worked vainly to save the tiny colt, who was little more than a month old.

When the vet told us he was beyond our help, we had him put to sleep (euthanized) beside his mother, where he stayed for the night. We had the body removed the next morning. Oskaloosa was left to grieve privately.

O'Sullivan Farms owner Randy Funkhouser was as sorry as the rest of us. To assuage our grief and disappointment he promised us a free breeding with his super West Virginia stallion Eastover Court.

As fate would have it, within the year the big gray, father of Confucius Say, two-time West Virginia Horse of the Year, was to die unexpectedly of a viral infection.

It was a terrible loss for Funkhouser and Oskaloosa's breeding partnership was staggering from its combined setbacks but the resolute breeder came through for us.

In 2005, Oskaloosa was bred to Way West, one of Funkhouser's most prolific sires, Randy's gift to our breeding group. The Way West progeny, due in April, 2006, turned out to be a healthy colt.

As I've said, most claimers don't stay with us very long, moving through in perhaps two to three months at most, so you don't get that emotionally involved with them.

The horses we breed are a different story. They stay with us for three to four years, sometimes more, and it can be heart-wrenching to see them go, try as I might not to get too close.

Some are keepers. We kept Probably's Devil close by. Marie Draus adopted him. His mother, Probably the One, was adopted by her groom, Amy Nicol, of Victor, NY, enjoying her retirement on the Nicol farm until she died in 2005.

BETTING

Chance is perhaps the pseudonym of God when he did not want to sign.

- ANATOLE FRANCE, *Le Jardin d'Epicure*

As any racetrack habitué will tell you, the rationale for betting on a particular racehorse often knows no bounds, dancing on the fringes of lunacy if not defying all reason. What else explains a bet made solely on the basis of a stable's colors?

I can hear the bettor's explanation now. "Let's see. The jockey is wearing green. That's the color of money. So, yeah, let's go with green, mother. Where's my purse?"

Not that there is anything wrong with that. Wild and crazy bets are part of the fun at the racetrack. There is just one important proviso. Don't get carried away. If you don't know what you're doing, do it in moderation.

Even the presumed experts have to tread carefully (sensible trainers, by and large, rarely bet) and there is of course no such animal as a sure thing.

For horse owners, there is another rule (or should be). Don't follow your heart. There is an almost overwhelming temptation inherent in horse ownership to wager heavily on your horse, and that is also true of shared ownership. But following your emotions rather than your head and your pocketbook can be a surefire way to lose.

Too often I've been dismayed to see one of our partners put himself in a big hole by betting more than he normally would because it was a Hampshire horse.

Our syndicate's win percentage is considered extraordinarily good by horsemen. Still, a 20 percent win ratio means that four times out of five, the Hampshire horse loses.

Having a first-rate partnership with a top trainer and a leading jockey can also be a drawback of sorts if it makes your horses prohibitive favorites.

One of our partners was to complain: "You can't win big when your horse leaves the gate at 4-5 odds."

It has been rare for us to have a horse compete at more than 4-1, and it's this point, if betting fairly big, that has proven the best occasion to take an emotion-driven flyer. One of our partners (the one I know about, anyway) bet big in the unusual instance of an 8-1 horse and in that single race recouped his entire investment in the Hampshire.

How about the "inside information" that comes with horse ownership? Well, occasionally one might pick up, usually in the paddock, some snippet about a horse that says it definitely will not be a winner. Even the greenhorn owner can spot the basic body language of a horse that is not ready. And eventually he begins to learn about bowed tendons, sore hocks, suspect suspensories, and cracked hooves - physical complaints not always apparent to the casual racegoer.

Being able to discard a couple of horses from a field helps somewhat, especially if you can omit one of the favorites. That, in my experience, is the best one can hope for from insider information, and it will still be a gamble when you place your bet. They don't call it "playing" the ponies for no reason.

Among our partners, there are some, even those entering as neophytes to horseracing, who quickly affect the style of the seasoned punter.

You'll find them with a folded copy of *The Daily Racing Form* under an arm, a pencil stub behind an ear, and binoculars hanging loosely around the neck.

They'll be talking to each other, often behind their hands, about "Beyers" (speed figures), past performances, "works," and fractions. Or they'll be discussing trainers and jockey changes and breeding and "first time Lasix."

I love it when some of the them actually use the information in "The Form" to make an intelligent wager.

A few of our partners have entered handicapping contests. Mike Dempsey of Pensacola, Florida, and Leland Keller of Fairfax, Virginia, gained exalted status when they won a couple.

Then there is "off-track betting" as practiced by Bill Verity, the Ohio steel baron who, at the time, was the U.S. Secretary of Commerce. Here is how that works:

I'm middle management at Commerce. Verity, a racing enthusiast, is the boss, and he's heard via the grapevine of our syndicate's activities - and that Duke Toby is scheduled to run his first race for Hampshire I.

Verity slips me a $20 bill and says, "Bet Duke Toby to win."

The Duke wins and I carry $50 around in a plain white envelope for a couple of weeks waiting for the appropriate time to give it to Verity.

The chance comes when Verity, appointed by President Reagan, now leaving with the election of the first Bush, is retiring as Secretary. We meet on a crowded elevator. I slip him the envelope. He knows what it contains.

He's a millionaire several times over but he still beams at winning fifty bucks by backing the Duke. It's our little secret.

Does betting on the ponies ever come anywhere near close to being a science?

Well, before you even think about that, let me tell you about my son, Malcolm, Jr., then aged 6, and his kindergarten teacher, Miss Ann, a.k.a. Ms. Ann Benfield, manager of DOT Day Care, Inc., a federal child care facility, in Washington, D.C.

I had invited them to join me and a large Hampshire partnership group filling two adjacent grandstand boxes at Laurel Park.

The Hampshire's ace at the time, Probably The One, the number six horse in the sixth race, won for us, and Malcolm, Jr. was given $5 (an admittedly measly share of the $6,000 purse winnings). He and Miss Ann accompanied us to the winner's circle licking on big ice cream cones and the kid got the bug.

The next race, he wanted to bet his $5 on the number six horse, arguing that since number six won in the sixth, it was only reasonable that number six would win again. Nothing could dissuade him.

Miss Ann, skilled in the art of compromise, put $2 of the kid's money on number six, who had been 20-1 on the morning line and was a staggering 99-1 on the tote board.

You know what happened. Number six won by a head and paid $164 for the $2.

Okay. Move on. Malcolm, Jr., now aged 7, is a jaded track habitué. We are with another large group of Hampshire partners, spouses and friends, again at Laurel.

Malcolm, Jr. is disinterested in the proceedings and has been sketching for an hour or so before glancing at my program and idly asking what my triple picks are in the next race.

Tim Feldman, a limited partner, turns the question around, asking the kid for his picks.

Malcolm, Jr. says number seven looks good, since there is a resemblance to a favorite cartoon character, Chip N Dale (the horse's name is Chip N Me). Number one looks good because it is named after a frog. Number fourteen definitely has something going for him on account of being named Funny Bear.

"Great reasoning," Tim says, noting that the frog and the bear are outlandish long-shots, while Chip N Me is the favorite.

Two minutes before post time Malcolm, Jr. reminds us that he was asked his opinion on the triple and had given his best opinion as to the exact one, two, three order of finish. Have I made the $6 wager? No, I haven't. Will I, please? Yes, I will.

It is further decided that his part of the take, if any, will be $55, a figure advanced by him.

Chip N Dale wins by a nose, the frog and the bear finish second and third, as required, and the triple pot is $4,500.

I am thoroughly chastened by the whole experience and it is made all the worse when the kid informs the teller that his share is $55. Much more than that happened to be earmarked for his college fund. But try to explain to a quizzical teller in the flush of the moment.

7
BAD DECISIONS AND GOOD HORSES

"A horse thou knowest, a man thou doest not know."

- TENNYSON, *Gareth and Lynette*

In 2002, we decided to phase out most of our claiming operations in Maryland to concentrate on our small breeding program with Oskaloosa, a modestly bred mare destined for the abattoir, and to buy privately young, un-raced horses from one of West Virginia's oldest and highly respected horse farms.

We formed a business association with O'Sullivan Farms, which was standing Black Tie Affair, Way West, Prized, and which had Housebuster before he died unexpectedly in 2005. Earlier, Eastover Court was the farm's best known stallion, siring Confucius Say which for two years was West Virginia's Horse of the Year.

After claiming or buying scores of horses for syndication, I was to privately purchase, for myself, one of Eastover Court's last progeny, a two-year-old gray filly named Marnie's Imperial. The opportunity came along when my son dropped out of college to enlist in the U.S. Air Force. I spent the money he saved me on the horse, as well as a brand new Lexus SUV.

I sent Marnie's Imperial, named for O'Sullivan Farms co-owner Ruth Funkhouser (her grand children call her Marnie, and this regal octogenarian likes a shot of Canadian Imperial whisky before bed time) to conditioner Dean Keller in South Carolina who would deliver her to trainer Dale Capuano to race in summer 2006 under my own name rather than that of the Hampshire, though I planned to use the pink and black Hampshire colors for the jockey's silks.

The idea of turning from claiming to private purchases for the Hampshire partnerships appeared to be a good one, but like every enterprise it is only as good as its weakest part. It was destined to fail for two reasons: the trainer we "borrowed" from our breeder friend, Randy Funkhouser, who with his Hawaii-born mother owned O'Sullivan, was in the habit of marching to his own tune and taking upwards of nine months to prepare our horses for the races, instead of what most other trainers took 45 to 60 days to do. Also, I walked smack into the inherent conflict of interest that occurred by using the O'Sullivan Farms' own trainer.

It was a naïve request on my part in the first place, resulting in our having no authority over the trainer, and his boss, Funkhouser, busy through 2005 with building a grand, new breeding shed for his stallions, having little time and no incentive to speed up the training process for us. The result, the overspending of tens of thousands of dollars for training that, in the end, was deemed neither satisfactory nor, in two instances, adequate.

These early experiences don't mean that what we did can't work in the future. We obviously learn by our mistakes, and, brother, was this a lulu. While you don't enjoy piling on, the failure had to be credited almost entirely to the trainer. My fault was not to have spotted, then acted upon, the weakness sooner.

The reason I didn't was because we did enjoy an early and significant success with a gelding named Three Aces, an "impulse buy" straight off the race track in the spring of 2004. This horse was brought to our attention during morning gallops at the Shenandoah Downs training track adjacent to Charles Town. He looked sharp, trainer George Yetsook said he was speedy and pretty much was ready for the track, and he was for sale. He was owned, of course, by his boss, Funkhouser. We did a bit of horse trading there and then; I lined up six potential partnership shares at $3,000 apiece on the spot, offered $18,000 to counter the asking price of $20,000, and we had ourselves our first horse. Randy, in fact, bought in for two shares, I took one, and sold shares to two of our directors, including Ray Duncan of Cross Junction, VA, and Don Morris of Emmitsburg, MD, and the last share to a Bunker Hill, WV, physician's wife, Mary Recht.

Within a week, we also did a deal with O'Sullivan for three more un-raced horses, including the fillies Moon Lust, a three-year-old, and two two-year-olds, a lovely Eastover Court gray named Karate Kat, and a Makin colt named Makin Moola. These cost $30,000, and I raised $65,000 as a result of a couple of symposia in Virginia and West Virginia, plus some word of mouth marketing. This trio was syndicated among 12 owners, again including myself. It is our policy that at least one of the Hampshire's top officers takes a position in each of the syndicated groups. Both Bill Joyce and I bought into these three horses.

Since Three Aces had already been broken--the three other horses were immediately sent to the South Carolina farm for breaking and early training--he was soon at the track, and after a slow start, running 6th on June 30th, then a lackluster 9th on July 16th, he surprised us with a 2nd place finish on September 5th and broke his maiden the following month. He won again, our 119th career win, in February 2005 and we were just as proud of his third place finish in a stakes race on that year's West Virginia Breeders' Classic XIX card in October. He won again to close out his 2005 campaign on December 11th, bringing his earnings to $63,352.

Karate Kat excelled in the three-horse partnership. She scored a fifth place in the classic, but it had taken a full nine months to get her to the races not including 45 days in "school" in South Carolina. She made up for lost time by posting impressive victories on July 16th and August 7th, and a second place in a stakes race on September 17th and earnings in her brief racing lifetime of $51,825.

So our entry into racing hitherto un-raced horses was working out pretty well. Unfortunately, Karate Kat's stable mates, Moon Lust, the three year old, now four, had fallen by the wayside, and had no discernable talent. She had earned but a few hundred dollars from three desultory races and was put up for adoption. Makin Moola suffered a throat ailment, went for surgery in June, was on the farm doing rest and rehab until December, and returned to South Carolina for 45 days of training in January 2006.

Which led Randy to suggest that perhaps the way to go was single horse syndicates.

Whatever, one thing that could not be allowed to happen was to involve a trainer in the planning of the partnerships, then have him do his own thing. In all cases, we asked for an approximate time estimate for when each horse could be expected to get to the track (i.e. begin racing). Not unreasonably, Yetsook appeared to us to stretch it a bit, giving himself four months or so. And that's what we budgeted, figuring the little extra time (most trainers we'd had experience with would give themselves 45-60 days with young horses which already had received considerable on-the-farm conditioning after breaking) would only benefit the horses and not put the trainer under undue pressure. A pattern began to develop of our horses coming up from "school" in South Carolina, then continuing in training for another 210-270 days *at $50 a day each*.

The last straw in this little game occurred when we were at O'Sullivan Farm in March 2005 to purchase another three youngsters for $25,000 (Double Toll Gate, Makin Mischief, Heavenly Cause) and found two older horses for sale that looked good for the $12,000 asking price.

Lovely Countess and Stillro Noki were a couple of four-year-old fillies who'd been to the training track, but somehow or other had been left behind, perhaps for unpaid bills, and Randy needed to unload them. At this point, we had a claiming partnership with about $8,000 in cash but no horses. We re-opened the partnership to sell several more shares to existing or new share owners to pay for the two new horses, aiming to pay for the two fillies' training with the $8,000 that already was in the bank. About 60 days was all that the trainer said he required to lick at least one of the two girls into racing shape. *Seven months and $21,400 later*, neither one of these horses had gotten to the races. In fact, neither one even had a gate card-- the equivalent of a driver's license if you own a car.

A gut feeling had told me months earlier that I should take a closer look at what was going on, and in July I made the decision to consign the Double Toll Gate group to another trainer, along with our home bred, Lunar Indian. But it took me until the end of October to send a van to pick up Lovely

Countess and Stillro Noki to deliver them to Dale Capuano at Laurel, along with the rest of the Charles Town-based horses. Each time I asked, Stillro Noki, particularly, would be at the track "next month," "next month," "next month."

Our partners were beginning to make fun of me at the track and on the Hampshire Hotline. The Hampshire was beginning to lose credibility, both George and Randy had, by this time, lost credibility with most all of the partners, with me, and members of my board. I was beginning to lose sleep. My doctor prescribed sleeping pills and anxiety medication. My wife advised me to quit. While it didn't seem worth the effort, I had to soldier on. We had 11 horses in our stable!

And, unfortunately, that wasn't the end of the story. Stillro Noki arrived at her new home with an unreported (to me) ankle injury and Lovely Countess required another five weeks training plus obtaining her gate card before she could be entered in her first race at Charles Town on December 23rd. As luck would have it, adverse track conditions caused the race to be cancelled, driving us further into the red, and prompting one of our partners to refer to her in 2006 as our "five year old virgin." Even worse was to befall this horse and this partnership: equine herpes virus, a highly contagious disease, broke out at Pimlico in January, 2006, and Maryland horses were prohibited from entering races at Charles Town, so Lovely Countess missed yet another race date on January 19th. The bills continued to mount.

The Stillro Noki/Lovely Countess training debacle strained relationships with the breeding farm operators, Randy and Ruth Funkhouser, and Clissie Funkhouser, Randy's wife and CPA book keeper, people who I had held in the highest regard. The Hampshire board cried foul because promised services had not been delivered, and the farm people responded that they weren't responsible for the time it took to train the horses. As this book was being written, a middle ground was being sought which would probably satisfy no one but would come closest to producing the fairest result for all concerned. Neither side wanted to resort to expensive court actions which both Randy and I agreed no-one could benefit from. The public relations fallout certainly would have been a disaster.

Our small breeding operation with Oskaloosa hadn't gone particularly smoothly either. I've written elsewhere about our mare losing two out of three foals. Her first, sired by Malibu Moon, took a long time to develop, but began his career splendidly, second his first time out, then winning a maiden special a month later. Unfortunately, Lunar Indian began to develop some problems in his front end (suspensory ligaments) immediately after, so we put him on the farm for the winter, hoping the rest would help him. Fortunately for his 10 owners, he'd won $22,816 from his two races, and with several thousand dollars due in owners and breeders bonuses in February, 2006, he had begun to pay his way, and helped also to pay the expenses of his mom, Oskaloosa, and the half-brother born in the spring.

You can see from the figures quoted above that there is definitely a possibility of making money on young horses if you are fortunate enough to choose right. You will also see that while three horses made all of the money, there are three more not yet producing and two that never will produce. A crap shoot, some say. I say its living just a little on the edge and you must be comfortable in taking an occasional tax loss when investing in thoroughbreds!

WHAT TO DO? BUY YOUNG, CLAIM, BREED?

Any color, so long as it's red,
  Is the color that suits me best,
Though I will allow there is much to be said
  For yellow and green and the rest.

- EUGENE FIELD, *Red*

Now that we've tried all three - buying un-raced horses, breeding for racing, and claiming - it's tempting to choose a favorite avenue. Let's say, however, that all three have their up sides, and all three have their down sides. But all three can be affordable - one of our favorite words - and most all of our more recent partners have tried each one. Let's ask a few of them.

Linda Wasilius of Martinsburg, West Virginia, a bank vice president: Breeding for racing is my favorite. Having your mare, picking the stallion, and waiting for the foal is the essence of racing. It's almost like having your own child when the foal is born.

Of course, you have to wait several years for that foal to run. It can be quite expensive to maintain the mare, pay the stud fee, and prepare the offspring until it is ready to race, perhaps at age 2, perhaps not until 3 or even 4. Many things may, and do, happen between birth and racing, so this is not the easiest path to racing, but it is the most fulfilling.

There is nothing in the world like seeing your homebred cross the finish line first, and walk into the winner's circle... believe me!

Ray Duncan of Cross Junction, Virginia, financial consultant: In the claiming business, you buy (claim) a horse from the current owner. The phrase "caveat emptor" comes to mind. If you choose this avenue, employ a trainer with a good record in the claiming business. This is the quickest way to get into ownership of thoroughbreds.

If you choose to purchase a horse that has never raced, you won't know how it will perform on the track. This unknown factor, however, adds to the excitement and anticipation, but you typically wait a while before your horse runs.

Breeding for racing takes a much longer time, perhaps two to three years, to see your horse at the track. Having experienced all three options over the past 23 years, my preference is to purchase a young, un-raced horse.

Kay F. Minton of Chantilly, Virginia, law office manager in Washington, D.C.: Breeding to race is, fundamentally, a crap shoot! The downside: you are looking at three-plus years from breeding to training to racing, not counting your initial foray into choosing and buying a brood mare and then choosing the stallion, with lots to go wrong during the gestation and after the foal hits the ground. Upside: Makes you feel like a proud parent. Summary: not for the impatient.

The upside of buying young horses for racing is that you get to see your horse develop from a weanling or yearling into a race horse. You direct how he is trained and how any health or lameness problems are handled. Downside: Getting them young, you don't know if they have the ability or desire to race and, of course, accidents or health problems can take them right out of the game before they even get started. Summary: Slower than claiming, but the finished product is yours.

The upside of claiming horses is that you jumpstart into racing. You get a horse that has gone through all the training, appears to have the ability to do his job, and is already racing. You could be getting a "diamond in the rough." Downside: You don't know his or her quirks or - major item - health problems. Summary: excellent and quick way to get into the business of horse racing.

Don Morris, Emmitsburg, Maryland: "Whatever your method of entering partnership horse racing - DO IT! It's a great hobby and it needn't be expensive. I tell my friends, "It costs less than playing golf!"

In my case, and the case of Bill Joyce, my first partner and co-founder of the Hampshire, we each have owned a horse of our own. The immediate downside of such a venture is expense. I remember this being Bill's complaint when he went solo, as a bachelor, in the 1980s - he's never tried it since he married Kathy - and I'm experiencing it now as I enter almost $1,000 a month (soon to be $1,800) in my ledger.

My lovely gray filly, the 3-year-old Marnie's Imperial, is my first individual purchase, and she is being broken and conditioned at Keller Stables' Farm in South Carolina.

Weighing the options, the buying and training of un-raced two-year and three-year olds, has become my favorite avenue of interest and challenge, and it was immediately popular with potential partners when I strayed from claiming at the millennium.

Buying horses privately first entered Bill's and my mind over in England a decade ago, at which time we were promised the services of one of that country's most respected bloodstock agents. I suppose a bloodstock agent is the first person to seek out in this country if you are to do it by the book. I didn't.

I'd already made friends with two of our area's best-known and trusted breeders, three actually since I must mention brothers Josh and Michael Pons of Country Life Farm in Maryland in the same breath, also Raymond (Randy) Funkhouser of O'Sullivan Farms in West Virginia.

Both these farms were started in the 1930s by the Pons boys' and Funkhouser's dads. Josh, Michael and Randy have carried on the family tradition and now raise some of the finest "affordable" - there's that word again - horses in the East. Once in a while, they pop a world beater (think Cigar).

Upon moving to within 30 miles of the Funkhouser spread, where we continued our second foray into breeding for racing, I built a relationship with Randy, resulting in the formation of three partnerships that supported seven of his horses, average purchase price approximately $10,000 each. On his part, Randy invested in each of the partnerships and helped pick the horses for me. Such was his reputation, I trusted him.

No blood stock agent; no veterinarian; no one in the pasture except Randy and me. We culled from the various bands of colts and fillies, he explained blood lines and conformations, pluses and minuses, winnowing down to perhaps five from which I was able to choose two or three, and if he thought I picked incorrectly, he'd tell me why, and I'd guess again!

Similarly, Josh Pons gave me excellent advice when we were seeking out stallions during our first breeding for racing program in the early 1990s. Two of three offspring from

Country Life stallions were winners at the track; it wasn't Josh's fault that another equally lovely foal died of a virus just a few months old.

By the time Carol and I had retired from the federal government and moved to rural Front Royal, Virginia, the Hampshire had completed 14 years of claiming some 100-plus horses, which had won almost 100 races. All were what we chose to call "affordable" claims, averaging about $8,500, and we'd been successful in that we would have a horse in the winner's circle at least 20% of the time. Our trainers and jockeys said this was a number they would love to achieve. But rarely, very rarely, did our partners take away more money from their investments than they put in.

The important memento they took home during these years was the winner's circle photo which I know graces the recreation room, the powder room, the office, the lobby of many homes and places of employment in the Washington/Baltimore metropolitan area. This is what the $2,500-$3,500 investment bought the partners, aside from the fun and the thrills of watching the horses race at the local tracks, or on those race courses in nearby states. While we rarely had a 'bankrupt' partnership, we returned as little as 25% of original investments, averaging over the years perhaps 50-60% of money invested. I called it "entertainment value," and believe very sincerely it to be the best value, dollar for dollar, anyone ever paid for a sporting event. Though you might make a case that those are expensive photographs!

The work first Bill and I, then Carol and I, put into building and then operating the Hampshire partnerships can hardly be imagined. In dollar terms, our return, we figured, did not exceed a dollar an hour.

Bill for years called the Hampshire in all its facets "a labor of love", and he does to this day, even though, with our entry into the more remunerative adventure (so far) of racing young horses, the potential returns to both investors and operators are much higher.

So while claiming sees many more horses and many more races for partners to attend, the racing of the two and three-year-olds we buy from O'Sullivan Farms has provided me, and some of the partners -and here, I stress "some" - far more returns for our invested dollars.

More importantly, it allows us to realistically dream of finding another Funny Cide with the potential to become a Derby contender, or, at the very least, a candidate for the West Virginia Classics.

You can dream the same dream with the $8,500 claimers, too, but optimistically rather than realistically. Mostly, the best you get is what you buy - a $8,500 claimer that provides, at most, a couple of trips to the winner's enclosure.

Out of our 100-plus horses in 14 years, we had two that were truly outstanding, Probably The One, a $6,500 mare who won slightly more than $100,000 by 1992 and became our poster girl after birthing four winning runners for the Hampshire, and Landler, winner of $118,975 and a 2003 National Claiming Crown race, in 2003.

Breeding is a separate avenue entirely. Breeding is for those of us with patience. It is a waiting game. It has more drawn-out anxiety than either of the other two avenues we have experienced. Also, it has more beauty, more serenity, more opportunity to enjoy and appreciate what nature offers us, the miracle of new life, the joy of watching our new baby, the gratefulness we feel to his mother, and to those who have taken care of her. It is also the most expensive.

Our poster girl, Probably The One
(photo by Richard Popkin, Hampshire partner)

I have talked to the 20 of my partners who took part in the two mares we have bred and all admit to stirrings within them they never thought they had, one of them the indescribable joy upon seeing a new, awkwardly leggy and tentative foal venturing, for the first time, out into the sunlight beside a protective mom.

Then the waiting game begins over again. And the worrying as the foal develops into a teen-ager, then to an almost full grown two-year-old, then a full-blown athlete (our baby) venturing on to the race track for the first time. As a parent, I know that our feelings are akin to watching your own kid at a high school track meet, walking nervously to the starting blocks for the 100-yard dash.

Many of us had to deal with the deaths of three lovely foals. I personally held one, just seven weeks old, as he was euthanized beside his mother. It was a crying moment. I vividly remember giving the go- ahead to put another to death, my voice breaking over the telephone as a doctor at the New Bolton equine hospital in Pennsylvania said there was little or no hope for Opie.

The up side? Oh, man. The up side is when we come to know these horses as we know our dog or our cat at home, and have pet names for them. Also, they often seem to know us. When they win their first race, they strut so proudly towards us, and we're so proud, too. These are the times I've seen the owners cry tears of happiness, tears of sheer joy.

Anyway, there it is, take your pick, or try them all. Stay within your means. Make it affordable, as the Hampshire has always tried to do. This was never intended to be a "how to" book. There are plenty of those out there, down to every excruciating detail.

Some are helpful, perhaps, but this is a learn-as- you-go game. It is subject to change daily. Even the most experienced hand, like my friend Randy Funkhouser, will run into something unexpected and completely new. So we owners must be ready to adjust to change, or be destined for failure.

In this book, we simply wanted to give others an inside look at our horses, our partners, our trainers, our jockeys, our grooms, their peccadilloes, their foibles, and how, by and large, both animals and humans have enjoyed their experiences as part of the Hampshire.

It's been a trip, I can tell you, and the animals and the people have been wonderful - most of them, anyway. Between them, I hope they made this book worth a quick read. They have certainly added an extra dimension to this last part of my life, and I thank all of them. Yes, quite a trip, and the journey isn't over yet.

OTHER ADVENTURES

I shot a rocket in the air
It fell to earth, I knew not where
Until next day, with rage profound,
The man it fell on came around.

- TOM MASSON, *Enough*

It is difficult to find anything in common with a leading figure in the thoroughbred industry, but I once shared a singular distinction with Michael Gill, winner of more money than any other horseman in North America.

This was in the winter of 2004/2005 when Gill had amassed $5 or $6 million (who is counting?) and Hampshire horses were averaging gross purses of about $100, 000 a year.

Gill was banned from Delaware Park, among other race courses, and I got kicked off of Charles Town Races & Slots, the Class II track in West Virginia.

I was never quite clear on why Gill was tossed out of Delaware (he denied all wrongdoing). My sin (and I also denied any wrongdoing) was complaining about what I considered unsafe racing conditions at Charles Town when the track was reopened after supposedly being renovated.

The Hampshire's Lucky Larue had taken a bad step in the muck and had to be retired forever from racing. He was one of 10 horses who had to be vanned off that October night.

It wasn't an isolated incident. Before the renovation, horses had been falling by the numbers for weeks during wet weather days, and Charles Town 's oval had been dubbed "the most dangerous track in the country" by a local vet, Maurice (Tim) Casey.

What truly annoyed was that Charles Town, not Laurel, was now our home race course, as Carol and I had moved to Front Royal after our retirement from the federal government. We were across the state line in Virginia but only 30 miles away from Charles Town, 100 miles from Laurel.

In my opinion the renovation had changed nothing, so I wrote a letter to Charles Town's owner, Peter Carlino, president of Penn National Gaming Inc., in faraway Wyomissing, Pennsylvania.

I complained, quite properly, I thought, that the track's upgrades had not alleviated the dangerous conditions, and that to van off 10 horses in one night amounted to a racing travesty.

"Unfortunately, given how the track now behaves, particularly in wet weather, the (upgrade) work was bungled and there seems to be consensus that it needs to be done over without delay. Otherwise, someone, or some animal, is going to be killed."

Carlino, protesting otherwise and saying the course was safe for horses and people, was furious at an upstart racing partnership daring to criticize his track. According to Jimmy

Hammond, Charles Town's racing secretary, Carlino called and ordered him not to accept any entries of Hampshire horses.

Feathers were also ruffled at the local level. Unfortunately, in going directly to Carlino, I had blindsided Charles Town's general manager, Richard "Dickey" Moore, and Penn Gaming's senior vice president, John Finamore. Both caught the heat and Carlino's feelings were not to be assuaged.

The wheel fell off the car and my banishment--or, technically, the banishment of the Hampshire's horses--lasted from November 2004 into late January 2005. Unintentionally, I became a poster kid for many disaffected employees and horsemen at Charles Town.

As it happened, the ban applied only to our horses trained in Maryland by Dale Capuano. I raced two West Virginia-bred horses with impunity while hiding behind a court injunction that trainer George Yetsook had won against Carlino. Carlino et al had tried to bar horses in Yetstook's care from racing because he was contravening the rules by not racing them often enough. An irony, given my later problems with the trainer.

My association with Yetsook and particularly with my breeder friend Randy Funkhouser turned out to be a major reason for Carlino's action against me. Funkhouser was forever ranting against track actions that he said were against the health, welfare and financial well-being of the horsemen - owners, breeders, trainers, vets, grooms, hot walkers, mutual clerks, office staff and anyone else that came to mind.

Finamore quietly questioned my association with these two gentlemen, although he agreed that I certainly had the right to do business with them, and that the friends I kept were my own business. However …

The standoff was broken when I gained a grudging respect for Finamore, whose sense of fair play came to the fore, and a friend of mine, Bill Christine, the Eclipse award-winning turf writer for the *Los Angeles Times,* since retired, made a cursory inquiry or two in his home state of Pennsylvania. A reasonably affable couple of meetings with Finamore and Moore resulted in my being reinstated.

The foo-foo-rah was to the Hampshire's ultimate benefit as the publicity helped to fill up partnership groups. More importantly, I got a better understanding of what made the track, and the people who run it, tick.

Things were running smoothly again when a completely forgotten interview with another respected turf writer, Bill Finley, conducted the previous December when everybody was mad at each other, came back to haunt me.

The February issue of the *Mid Atlantic Thoroughbred* magazine carried a story headlined **Charles Town: A Track Divided**.

It quoted me as saying, "I don't like being played with like they played with us. What (track management) has done to us is unfair. And we haven't done anything wrong."

It was back on the carpet. Happily, apart from some hurt feelings, nothing changed, and the Hampshire continued racing all its horses at Charles Town, unimpeded. Dickie Moore even bought dinner for my wife and me.

This is not to suggest that all of my experiences as a horseman have been fraught with confrontation. In fact, racing opens unlikely doors, and once you pass through, you can have - here's the Englishman in me coming out - what I used to call a jolly good time.

Honeymooning in Rio de Janeiro, for instance, and this while merely a limited partner in one of my earlier ill-fated ventures, I managed to impress the hell out of new bride Carol at the Hippodrome Race Track.

I merely introduced myself as a Maryland owner and we immediately found ourselves in the horsemen's dining room with crisp white table cloths, linen napkins, complimentary champagne, and our own betting window.

Carol could hardly believe it. After all, at the time I owned just a small part of Grundoon, and he was broken down on a farm, not actually racing.

She whispered to me as we ate a fancy lunch: "What if they ask about your horses? You can't tell them you don't have any."

In fact, we were left quite alone. Everyone smiled a lot, spoke in Portuguese, and did what race trackers do everywhere: perused their version of the *Racing Form* and minded their own business.

Later, in March, 1990, while visiting England, I got mixed up for a while with some royals, and almost managed to put together an international version of the Hampshire.

One of my cousins, Don Charity, introduced me to Frank Osgood, the venerable racing secretary at Newbury Race Course, and Osgood said I ought to talk to Harry Herbert. Harry, described as a "fellow owner of thoroughbred stock," might have some ideas on how we could expand the Hampshire.

Osgood, well into his 70s, very much the English gentleman, was most eager to help Don's cousin from the colonies.

"Yes," he said genially, picking up a black dial telephone. "Mr. Herbert might find some time to chat with you. He's very fond of you Americans. I'll make sure he knows you're here."

The wheels were put in motion and Harry invited Charity and me to lunch at Kennet Valley Thoroughbreds, in Highclere Park, Berkshire.

Harry, a towering young man of 6 feet, 6 inches, and about 30, met us at the door of his office in a single-story, unimpressive building behind the very imposing Highclere Castle. We enjoyed sherry before a roaring fire and then repaired to a small dining room to enjoy roast lamb with two attractive young ladies from the office.

Hampshire director Tim Feldman of North Carolina and Malcolm Barr in the required top hat and morning suit for Royal Ascot 1999 meet in England.

Lunch over, Harry offered a tour of the castle, and partway through we came upon Harry's older brother, Geordie. We discovered, upon being introduced, that Geordie was known to less intimate friends as Lord Porchester, and, more importantly (to me, anyway), his and Harry's father, Lord Carnarvon, was Queen Elizabeth's racing manager.

Yes, Harry was a "fellow owner," but his thoroughbreds ran in the Arc de Triomphe, the Epsom Derby and the Rothman's Cup, all multimillion dollar races for the top horses in Europe.

I should perhaps mention here that Lord Carnarvon's grandfather, George Herbert, the 5th Earl of Carnarvon, financed the evacuation of King Tut's tomb, exposing treasures unsurpassed in the history of archeology.

His sudden death several months later lent credence to the story of the "Mummy's Curse" but was most probably explained by blood poisoning progressing to pneumonia after accidentally shaving a mosquito bite infected by erysipelas, a streptococcus skin infection more commonly known, at the time, as St. Anthony's Fire. Howard Carter, the earl's chief archeologist, and thereby the man most responsible for revealing the tomb of the young king, lived safely for another 16 years. Harry, incidentally, showed us some of the King Tut treasures at Highclere.

Anyway, in another surprise, Harry offered the Hampshire the services of his brother-in-law, John Warren, the queen's bloodstock agent and one of the best-known spotters of good horseflesh in the country. Warren, married to Harry's sister, Lady Caroline, was to be our agent in England if and when we launched a Hampshire International Partnership.

Our intention was to transfer older horses from England for racing in Maryland and this was duly reported by the *Daily Racing Form*. Unfortunately, we chose the 1990 recession to launch the endeavor, and while our ads in the *Wall Street Journal* and other business publications drew an unprecedented number of inquiries, our trainer Dale Capuano stood poised with new passport in hand, we could raise but half of the required capital. Our royal bubble burst.

Harry, who calls himself "half-American" (he spent three years in Kentucky, learning the American thoroughbred business, and his mother, Lady Carnarvon, is the sister of former U.S. Senator Malcolm Wallop, the Wyoming Republican), called on us the following year when he came over for the Turf Classic at Laurel.

We lunched at the National Press Club and talked briefly about what might have been.

Years later, Harry smoothly turned the tables, sending a letter inviting me into his Royal Ascot Racing Partnership.

Impressed, I showed the letter to Hampshire partner Tim Feldman, and we agreed to join, splitting the $16,000 cost.

Two years later, in the prerequisite top hat and tails, I was at Epsom Downs, where I watched our Derby horse Brancaster, jointly owned by some 300 other Royal Ascot partners, finish 11th in a field of 16.

That signaled the end of my fling in the high-end of racing. I returned home to watch the Hampshire's Indian Sprout, trained by Jeff Runco, win a $2,500 claiming race on the Fourth of July at Charles Town. It was an equally satisfying experience.

10
RACETRACKS

Heart of my heart, O come with me
To walk the ways of Arcadie.

- NORAH M. HOLLAND, *Grasshopper's Song*

We all have our favorite race courses. Unfortunately, mine is long gone, but, as my tattered, 20-year-old T-shirt, decorated with a tombstone, says, "not forgotten." The shirt is a relic of Maryland's racing past, Bowie Race Course, about 10-miles distant from its surviving upstart neighbor, Laurel Park.

They did most things wrong in building Bowie. One, they faced the grandstand into the afternoon sun, so you could scarcely see the races on a summer afternoon. They let it languish--among tracks, it was forever sort of an inner city slum, but with charm. It was the first in the country to host year round racing. From the late 1940s, the trains, many of them originating in New York City, discharged passengers almost at its gates come rain, snow or shine, 364 days of the year. Maybe they raced Christmas Day, I don't remember.

The grandstand was tatty, the food awful, the clubhouse dusty, and washrooms, well, they were useable.

But everyone who attended loved dear old Bowie. We called the apron in front of the grandstand Bowie Beach, took off our shirts, popped a cold one from our cooler, and settled back to sunbathe. Couldn't see the races anyway. The Hampshire never raced a horse there. The track was closed before we opened.

We did train over the track, though, and it always had an excellent surface. The jockeys loved it. And we stabled our first horses on Bowie's back side. Duke Toby, Super Operator, Foolish World. Our 25-year-old rookie trainer, Dale Capuano, had his dingy little office there. But we raced our horses over at spiffy Laurel where, when Joe DeFrancis took over management from his dad, we were prohibited from removing our shirts, taking in our own beer coolers, and generally making ourselves comfortable on the apron, now with our backs more comfortably to the sun.

In later years, when Magna Inc., the Canadian conglomerate, assumed control of Laurel Park, they tarted it up some, but it never had the feel of old Bowie Race Course. It did have in common an excellent dirt racing surface, and Magna also established a superior turf course that attracted large fields and expanded wagering.

While Charles Town in West Virginia is generally regarded as a pretty poor racing surface, the question is often asked, and John Finamore, a senior vice president for Penn National Gaming Inc., asked it of me during one of our discussions: "If you don't like the track, why do you insist on racing here?"

Well, the brief answer is: "Money." Most of the purses at Charles Town, since the introduction of slot machine gambling, are among the highest in the mid-Atlantic area. Also, for the spectator, the tiny, half-mile track 70 miles from Washington, D.C., allows the fans to get close to the horses, literally smelling the action, the sweat, and well, the manure. You get the idea.

We have hopes that Penn National Gaming Inc., which owns the track, will one day install an all-weather racing surface that should solve most of the problems produced by the current, less than satisfactory, racing surface, by standing up to the adverse weather of West Virginia winters.

In neighboring Maryland, the resident horsemen have been thwarted by politics in their bid for slots for years, and purses have gradually eroded to where many of us can hardly afford to race our horses there. For example, in 2005, the Hampshire had moved all of its horses to West Virginia. At year's end, due to the demand by a group of frustrated suburban and city racing enthusiasts around Washington, D.C., we opened one of our "affordable" claiming partnerships to race there, at Pimlico, and Delaware. We first claimed a $5,000 horse, Isn't True, which shortly was to be retired, without even hitting the board, to CPA Ed Roller's 7-acre farm in Harrisburg, VA, where he's now the family pet and renamed Chessie. Then came the dark brown colt Lively Sweep, a $7,500 claim, who sprang to life after palate surgery, won at $10,000 claiming and proceeded up the ladder to allowance company shortly thereafter.

Lively Sweep wins at Pimlico in May 2006. (Photo by Laurie Asseo, Hampshire partner)

Also at year's end, a training debacle caused us to move all our horses back to Maryland, but gradually, after finding a new conditioner, we've re-established our presence in West Virginia.

Laurel is really the jewel in the Maryland crown insofar as tracks are concerned. Pimlico, home of the Preakness, the second leg of the Triple Crown, is Maryland's other racetrack (aside from Timonium which runs for a week or so around Labor Day in conjunction with the Maryland State Fair), and some say it is doomed to eventual closure. It is a dilapidated plant, more than 100 years old, getting a few dabs of paint each year to spruce it up a bit before the Preakness Stakes the third Saturday in May when more than 100,000 people descend on it. A few years ago, the entire electricity system gave out for about half the card. One of our partners took a heart attack in the early summer heat. He recovered, but has since died. Pimlico, though the most historic, is the least attractive and uncomfortable of any track we race at, or that I have ever attended.

It contrasts sharply with Colonial Downs in the neighboring Commonwealth of Virginia, home of the immortal Secretariat, who never was able to race before a crowd of hometown fans for lack of a race track in Virginia until the late 1990s. Colonial Downs, sometimes compared to Saratoga in upstate New York, also prides itself on its turf courses. It holds a fairly short, but ever expanding, 45-day meet in mid-summer, and gains popularity each year. In 2006, its Virginia Derby maintains a firm foothold as a Grade II race with a $1 million pot. Colonial Downs, a stone's throw from historic Colonial Williamsburg, and about 20 miles east of the state capitol, Richmond, is a track where many, including an increasing number of Hampshire partners, like to overnight at local motels, hotels and historic bed and breakfasts.

Delaware Park is another visitor friendly track less than 100 miles from Washington D.C., and about 70 miles from neighboring Maryland tracks. Delaware was on its financial knees when slots were approved by the state about 12 years ago. Since then, it, too, has become a popular venue for horsemen with better than average horses. Purses there are even better than Charles Town, about 180 miles distant. Maryland, you see, is caught in the middle, and will be, even more so, when Pennsylvania, with its Penn National Race Course, near the capitol, Harrisonburg, and Philadelphia Park, get their slot emporia established in 2007.

Hampshire races its horses pretty regularly in all of these places, but most often in West Virginia and Maryland. On weekends, we get a pretty good group of followers to the out-of-town venues, many to enjoy the change of scenery.

As I write this, a dreadfully serious and virulent disease, equine herpes virus, has struck at Pimlico. Two horses are dead; eleven are ill. Maryland-based horses, even those we have stabled at Laurel, 30 miles away, are prohibited from racing out of state, so we had to race our West Virginia-bred maiden, Lovely Countess, in a $12,500 claiming race at Laurel instead of at Charles town. The purse was $10,000 and she was second, receiving $2,100. Had she been able to keep her race date in Charles Town, the purse for second was $8,000. Likely she would have won the entire pot against lesser competition (about $18,000). There's why we continue racing at Charles Town, Mr. Finamore!

11
THE DARK SIDE

"Trouble rides behind and gallops with him."

- BOILEAU, *Epitres*

For me, thoroughbred racing is the joy of my life, but there also can be a dark side, such as when a horse is injured and must be euthanized or when a foal dies despite heroic efforts to save it.

And while you can't expect a horse to win all of the time, when one of your best goes to the post as a runaway favorite, supposedly a lock, it can be really embarrassing when it loses very, very badly. Like coming in last.

I've seen it all over the years. There have been races I'd give anything to run again - or not to have run at all. And, along with my partners, I've been heartbroken by the loss of several foals.

I don't know which experience is worse, losing a horse or losing a foal. Perhaps the former. With a foal, you have some warning, which permits you to prepare for the inevitable. Losing a horse on the track can come with a speed that has you totally blindsided.

All Laughter, a misnamed 3-year-old claimer on which we had pinned our highest hopes, brought us one of our darkest moments.

Our sixth partnership group, The Hampshire Ascot, paid $8,500 for him, and in six times out the 3-year-old brown gelding was in the money five times, including two wins.

So it would be a gross understatement to suggest we were super confident when we decided to hold our December, 1991 annual meeting at Laurel, rather than at our regular venue in downtown Washington, the National Press Club, to coincide with one of his races.

All Laughter faced fairly lackluster competition and was the morning line favorite. Jockey Edgar Prado was the meet's winningest jockey. How could there be a better time to break with the Press Club tradition?

Over box lunches, we reported on the success of our partnership concept, introduced trainer Capuano for a questions and answers session, held a drawing (for monogrammed shirts and sweaters), and then headed, with great enthusiasm, for the betting windows.

Bill Joyce and I anticipated a record crowd in the winner's circle.

Then disaster struck. In a perverse twist of fate, All Laughter began pulling up on the turn, never to finish the 6-furlong race. We watched through binoculars in horrified silence while our champion was loaded into a horse ambulance.

Capuano reported that All Laughter had taken a bad step and seriously injured the suspensory tendons in his left leg. He likely would never race again.

We gave him away to a farm that pledged to take care of him at its expense, but when he didn't recover sufficiently in a few days, he was humanely destroyed and buried at the site of his brief new home. Several of our horses had developed serious ailments over the years but All Laughter was the first to succumb to a track-related injury.

The sorrow aside, it was the worst of times from a business standpoint. The Ascot partnership had gone from a potential positive cash standing of $12,000 - the value of the race, plus $6,000 if it had won - to a zero dollar value in less than two minutes.

With a capitalization of about $35,000, that's a hit you can't take very often, and it left an otherwise healthy partnership struggling for its life.

The Hampshire came close to losing Ima Social Climber in a different kind of mishap, this time in the stable area, after she had gotten loose from her stall. The 4-year-old filly, relatively undistinguished but at $6,500 something Capuano thought he could turn around, came to us in September, 1992.

We had raced her a couple of times, once finishing third, giving us hope, and once trailing last past the finish line, when Capuano reported in his usual understated manner that she had suffered a puncture wound in the left hock in a fall on hardtop.

Ima was taken from training and placed on antibiotics with a daily visit from the vet. Her next racing date - and therefore her next paycheck - stretched ever further into the future.

Bill Joyce and I became curious when we overhead gossip in the track kitchen indicating Ima's fall was more than routine, rather it had come about during almost two hours of virtual frenzy around shed row.

Thirty stable hands from the Capuano barn and neighboring facilities had risked life and limb as they endeavored in vain to secure our frightened horse as she galloped every which way on the Laurel backstretch. In the process, she fell to the ground several times, escaping mainly with superficial grazes, but also suffering the deep and serious puncture wound on her lower right leg, and was caught only when exhausted.

She had gotten loose because a stable hand had failed to put a restraining chain in place.

We tried not to attach blame, though we later learned the employee was fired. An incident is bound to happen occasionally when you are caring for up to 50 animals weighing well over half a ton apiece. Still, this was more horrific than most.

Ima was nursed back to health, apparently none the worse for her rampage, but it was a costly experience for the owners. She won, once at Delaware Park and at Penn National the following April and May, but went downhill after that and was sold privately with another has-been named Infrastructure for $10,000 the pair.

After the Ascot partnership lost All Laughter, we ultimately merged it with the Hampshire Curragh, which was undersubscribed during the 1991-92 recession years and was to suffer its own disaster at Laurel in July, 1992, with a brown filly named Leehawk.

The situation was eerily similar. Leehawk, claimed for $8,500 about a month earlier, was tipped as a winner in <u>every</u> newspaper covering Laurel, including the *Daily Racing Form*, the *Baltimore Sun* and the *Washington Post.*

In her first outing for the Curragh, the 4-year-old, moving up in class, had lost the narrowest possible photo finish, so close that we ordered the official photograph for the partnership archives as a memento. It took the stewards five minutes to figure out the winner, although we noticed early that our jockey, Edgar Prado, had unsaddled and weighed in long before the numbers flashed on the tote board. A top jockey evidently can tell, even if the loss - or the win - is by the proverbial eyelash, and this was.

At any rate it bode well. Under the excellent care of Erline, a favorite groom, Leehawk began to look like a million-dollar horse in her stall, and we all looked forward to her next time out.

But as luck would have it, we couldn't find a similar race for her, so we had to drop her in class, to $8,500 claiming, which is what we had paid for her. Capuano was fairly certain we would lose her at that price but she wasn't earning any money standing in her stall.

Our decision to race her was strictly monetary. We had gotten that second-place purse. We had an almost certain win in the offing at the lower level. If she was claimed, we'd still have a profit, which is the name of the claiming game.

Race day was bright, sunny and cool, no humidity yet in an unusually pleasant summer, and although it was a Tuesday, a number of partners had played hooky from their offices to see the race, wager more than the usual amount of money, and get their picture taken in the winner's circle.

We were an assured lot in the paddock. We sauntered around, we owners, racing programs tucked in our pockets, nonchalantly chatting with our jockey, Edgar Prado. Leehawk strutted, very much "on the muscle," ready to do her job.

Capuano told Prado: "Take her to the front and get what you can out of her. We won't have her after today."

Leehawk cantered confidently down to the post, the partners strolled confidently to the windows, and we settled back to wait confidently for the inevitable win.

It didn't happen. Leehawk failed to break on top. In fact, she broke a bit sideways, ran third and fourth for a while, and then turned it in for another day, apparently not liking to be behind other horses. Instead of challenging the front runners, she jogged in last in a field of eight, looking like she was out to enjoy the weather.

What an embarrassment!

"Well," I said, clearing my throat, "she's the other guy's problem now ... " - a reference to the public address announcement confirming her claim by another owner.

One of our group, also seeking solace, was sure she had run with a bad ankle, and soon he had everyone agreeing that the claim was for the best.

I quietly quizzed Capuano on the theory.

"What ankle injury?" he demanded. "She just didn't get out of the gate the way she should have and decided not to run. Probably didn't like the dirt in her face from the horses in front."

I was sorry I had asked.

The Ascot/Curragh joint venture briefly proved to the benefit of both, with R.T. Rise N Shine posting a win for both groups of partners.

When we sold R.T., however, the Ascot partnership was in hiatus, having no horses to watch. That's about the worst scenario you can imagine for any group of horse enthusiasts.

For several weeks we tried desperately to claim an animal but at this point Maryland thoroughbred stock was at an all-time low and we couldn't find a halfway decent horse in our cash bracket of about $8,500. It was yet another symptom of the 1986 tax act combined with the recession and, some said, poor breeding farm management that sent scores of operations into bankruptcy. We finally cashed out the members of the two partnerships after a two-year run.

Foolish World, a lightly raced, 3-year-old grandson of Kentucky Derby winner Foolish Pleasure, was another big disappointment for us.

He had broken his maiden only a couple of months before with young Kent Desmoreaux aboard and we were able to claim him for a bargain $20,000 after he finished fifth in a $40,000 allowance race. Despite that loss, he looked like every owner's dream, a potential stakes winner.

Unfortunately, while looking good in the mornings, Foolish World didn't show much on the track, either dirt or grass. Then he developed a sore throat.

For several weeks he was treated for an infection by his veterinarian. Well again, we sent him off to race, but it rained that day and we had to scratch. Among his other foibles, Foolish World disliked getting his feet wet.

In growing desperation, we sent him to Atlantic City, where, after driving 200 miles, we waited until past midnight to watch him run fourth in a field of 10 on an evening card.

Even more desperate, we removed his blinkers, and, *Voila!*, he turned in his best performance for us at Delaware Park, running two-fifths of a second off the track record but still placing third in a photo behind two front-running speedballs.

Not bad. Maybe, just maybe, we had the answer. Not so, said his groom, Erline. Foolish World, she insisted, was wrong in the head, and she was right.

He finished fifth on the turf at Philadelphia Park (enough to pay the van bill, since fifth place gets a check) and in his last race for us, at Laurel, he broke in the middle of the pack and finished there.

It was a $5,000 claiming race and no one claimed him. A few days later, we sold him privately for $1,500, an $18,500 loss on the original purchase price.

In six months Foolish World had virtually bankrupted our second partnership. We made a halfhearted attempt to revive Hampshire II with a $5,000 horse, Due It Smoothly, but the best Smoothly was able to manage in nine races for us was a win at another second-grade track, Penn National. We left him there and eventually sold him locally for $1,000.

Lesson learned: don't hang on to unsuccessful horses. In Foolish World's case, six months was far, far too long.

In the twelfth year of our operations, with the early exception of All Laughter, we had escaped a serious injury among almost 100 horses that had passed through our stables.

Then, in the summer of 2000, with an unprecedented eight horses racing, all four of our partnerships were plagued with injuries and illness.

My Boy CK bowed a tendon racing at Delaware Park. Oskaloosa was found to have serious ligament damage in her left knee after we claimed her from a winning race in Maryland. Rammer suffered self-inflicted deep cuts at the back of her ankles after she "grabbed a stifle" (cut the back of her forelegs with her rear hooves) in a race at Pimlico. St. Mo had severe pulmonary bleeding in his first race at Laurel. Hampshire Dancer underwent surgery for bone chips in her right rear ankle.

My Boy CK was retired. Oskaloosa, retired as a brood mare, produced a healthy first foal, but her two other offspring brought us tragedy, as detailed in the chapter on breeding.

Yes, thoroughbred racing is the joy of my life, but there is a dark side.

12
TRAINERS

All our progress is an unfolding, like the vegetable bud. You first have an instinct, then an opinion, then a knowledge.

- EMERSON, *Essays, First Series: Intellect*

We have men in all sizes, as a friend of mine says, when he's hustling clothes for charity. The same goes for trainers. There's a wide range of them.

The Hampshire has experienced quite a spectrum over the years, profiting with the best, doing so-so with some, and getting burned by others.

From the start, we've had Dale Capuano, who is top of the line, guiding the bulk of our partnerships. He has been the major factor in the partnerships' success.

When, for various reasons, we've used other trainers, the results have been mixed, and a couple - by my measure, at least - were disasters.

As I mentioned earlier, Larry Lacey, an old friend of mine, recommended Capuano to me and me to Capuano, so going into business with him was something of an arranged wedding.

For us, it was a fortuitous combination. For example, in 2001, Capuano ranked fourth in the nation with 235 victories and $4.4 million in earnings. In 2003, Mid Atlantic Thoroughbred magazine had a cover story calling him "A Legend in the Making," and in 2005, he won his eighth Maryland training title in nine years.

Of the 100 or so horses he has claimed and trained for the Hampshire, most have been in the $8,500 range, and he has improved many to run at $12,500, some in allowance company, which is a major step up in class from the claimers we usually competed. Allowance horses may not be claimed and usually run for higher purses.

We've also watched Capuano drop just as many others in at $5,000, often to be claimed away. To his credit, only a half dozen have been retired due to injury, and only one, through December 2005, has been vanned off the track.

The Hampshire's win ratio, after 559 races, has been 21% over 17 years. To December 31, 2005, these were our on-the-board statistics:

Races	Win	Place	Show	Fourth
559	120	77	69	72

Capuano is that rare breed who knew what he wanted to do with his life at age ten and managed to do it exceedingly well in a highly competitive field at a relatively young age. The "kid" (he was 25 when we met him) had the advantage of coming from solid racing stock. His father, Philip, was a breeder and did some training, and Capuano has now joined him on the Maryland Thoroughbred Horsemen's Association board, where he is active as a negotiator with track management. His uncle,

Louis, Philip's brother, was a trainer who did some breeding, while Capuano's brother, Gary, is a trainer, and his cousin, Nick, is an assistant trainer. It's obviously in the blood.

Dark and handsome, Capuano is a taciturn guy, soft spoken, and a bit difficult to communicate with. You have to know what questions to ask to get the answers you want and it took me a few years to find a comfort zone but we're good now.

He is very dependable and has a great work ethic in what is a family affair. Married, but separated in 2006 from wife, Ally, who rode the difficult horses for him in the morning, he now relies on one principal assistant, John Brady. Before marrying a trainer and moving to Canada, his sister, Gina, used to be his similarly capable assistant.

Capuano usually has about 60-80 horses under his care and makes a hands-on inspection of every horse on a daily basis. They are paraded in front of him in the morning by their grooms (each has charge of three to four horses). He runs his hands down each leg, feels each knee and ankle for "heat," and then relays his findings to an assistant, who is standing by with a yellow legal pad. He orders any medications, poultices and bandages that may be necessary. Somehow, he makes his wishes known to the groom, who generally is an Hispanic, English limited.

For my part, I give him a mid-morning cellular call three or four times a week, checking on our horses, but other than that he has a free hand. I visit the stables infrequently.

I am told that few trainers are more fastidious than Capuano in their personal attention to the animals. Certainly few horses on the Maryland circuit are so well groomed and otherwise turned out than those wearing the blanket of the Dale Capuano Racing Stable.

We did have one rough period with Capuano. Bill and I almost fainted when we saw an ad in the *Daily Racing Form* announcing establishment of a $1 million racing syndicate in Maryland. Normally we wouldn't have worried. We knew that kind of high-rolling operation would never fly in our neck of the woods.

But Capuano, *our* trainer, according to the article, had not only invested in the new outfit, he was on the board of directors. We called foul.

In our opinion, this was blatant conflict of interest. Capuano knew virtually every aspect of our small enterprise. How could he objectively look after our interests while having a management role in a competing syndicate?

Our worst fears were realized when the new syndicate managed to raise only about the same capitalization as the Hampshire. Now, rather than being a grandiose operation, fielding horses beyond our reach, it was competing on our level, trying to make inroads into the market we had taken three years to penetrate and nurture.

With Capuano on the board, its horses soon had to be juggled around so as not to compete directly with ours, and vice versa. Capuano professed not to be influenced by this dilemma but our partners were livid. Okay, they ranted, maybe there's no malfeasance, but this certainly looks like a bad case of naiveté.

Briefly, we looked for an alternative trainer, but it was apparent that Capuano was the best around, not only a top handler but canny at spotting good claims and opportune races to run them. We would only be harming ourselves if we parted company. In three years, we'd had 36 wins with him. Besides, we really liked the guy.

I found consolation in buying a voodoo doll and sticking pins in it. Apparently that worked. In the next six months, we scored 10 wins, while the new outfit struggled to get just one.

Eventually, and in only a short time, the new outfit went out of business. We rubbed salt in the wound by asking to buy their mailing list - for pennies on the dollar.

Interestingly, at a Thoroughbred Owners and Breeders Association (TOBA) symposium in the late 1990s, respected trainer Michael Dickinson spoke out against trainers establishing their own partnerships, suggesting they should have enough to do in tending to the business of training. His was not a popular position among his colleagues, but, in my opinion, it was the correct one.

When we have strayed off the reservation, racing at other tracks on a consistent basis, not just a one shot, as with Landler at Canterbury Park, we mostly go with trainers at those tracks, rather than haul our horses back and forth from Laurel, and earlier from Bowie.

In our first out-of-state venture, Bill and I traveled to Philadelphia Park in March, 1993, looking around at the behest of one of our partners, Mark Hytowitz, who lived in the area. We talked to people in the stands as well as around the backside and settled on our first woman trainer, Pam Shavelson.

Pam, having served a long apprenticeship with the Mark Reid stable, rising from lowly groom to a top assistant, was at that time among the half dozen top trainers in Philadelphia. She had been on her own for about five years and had some 30 horses in her stable. She also had a reputation as the kind of hands-on trainer we had come to admire.

With few women jockeys in the business, and even fewer women trainers, we felt that we had broken some new ground, and many of our partners, especially the younger set, were excited about having Pam. Bill and I also had an ulterior motive. Our successes had been spotty recently and we felt that any positive distraction would help pull us through the bad times.

Capuano didn't seem too happy with us, but we took our filly Intoxicated, who wasn't having a very good time of it in Maryland, and shipped the three-year-old to Pam.

After showing such a dislike for racing surfaces at Laurel and Pimlico, Intoxicated enjoyed immediate success with Shavelson, winning the first time out and finishing in the money eight of the ten times she raced at Philadelphia, including another trip to the winner's circle.

During our stay at Philadelphia, Bill authorized Pam to pay $7,500 for another horse, an un-raced three-year-old roan gelding (I can take no credit, again vacationing in Hawaii, where I had started life in the United States back in 1961), and this brought us full circle in the City of Brotherly Love.

Purchased in August, 1993, it took a while to get Jan's Special to the races, and then he was not fond of the gate. He was left trailing and out of the money on three occasions. Finally, just before Christmas, he scored a long-shot first place, giving us a nice present, a $3,000 purse, and ending the year on a winning note.

This was our 11th win that year, producing an enviable 25% winners (43 horses ran), our highest win percentage in five years of racing. Over that 5-year period, competing 220 times, we had an impressive 21% win, 66% on-the-board average. In 1991, our busiest year, we sent 66 horses postward, winning 14 times.

Intoxicated's string of victories and Jan's Special's surprise win shielded a bad period for us at tracks in Maryland and illustrated the importance of constantly trying new things - if only to distract partners' attention from where the bombs are falling.

Unfortunately, Jan's Special never produced again for the Hampshire, and he was sold privately, to a partner, for $3,000. He was to never win another race and effectively ended our syndicate's eighth limited partnership. We left Pam and Philadelphia regretfully. It turned out to be too distant a stable to be practical for us.

The Hampshire again used a woman trainer, Claudia Gillions, in our first foray into Charles Town in West Virginia, but this was short-lived and disastrous.

Her first claim for the Hampshire broke down before reaching the finish line, requiring euthanasia.

Next, we used the affable Jeff Runco, Charles Town's perennial top trainer, only to achieve indifferent results. Maybe we expected too much, but Runco, a great trainer, never seemed to have much of an eye for a decent claim. Though he scored a few winners for the Hampshire, after a couple of years it was time to move on.

Casey Dunkelberger, the lovely young wife of Travis Dunkelberger, a leading jockey who rode regularly for us, also tried her hand at training for the Hampshire, but bad luck kept her out of the winner's circle, not lack of trying.

One difficult challenge we gave Casey was to take one of our homebreds, Probably's Devil, out of retirement. He hadn't raced for two years after suffering a leg injury while losing to future "Horse of the Year" Evening Attire at Saratoga. Before that, he'd raced five times, won twice, was second twice.

Casey got him as far as a second place finish at Penn National. Unfortunately, the reclamation project foundered there, and the Devil was put back to pasture, which he enjoyed more than racing

After Casey, the Hampshire entered a new phase, deleting claiming from its business plan for the time being and concentrating on the purchase of young horses, two-and three-year-olds, from the O'Sullivan Farms in Charles Town.

This was an exciting idea but it brought us to our financial knees. Our new trainer, George Yetsook, perhaps wanting to bring only "perfect" horses to the track, took a prohibitively expensive, for our rapidly expanding but modestly funded group of partnerships, length of time to get our horses to the races. We also felt quite strongly that in our league there was no such animal as the "perfect" race horse.

This isn't to say that some great things didn't happen. The five horses we first purchased were well-bred but relatively inexpensive, with most of them competitive in the allowance ranks, a higher echelon than we normally competed.

In 2005, two of them, Three Aces, a four-year-old gelding, and Karate Kat, a handsome, three-year-old gray filly, were entered in stakes races in Charles Town's biggest race night of the year, the West Virginia Breeders' Classics XIX. Three Aces actually hit the board, taking third place, making us feel very proud of this maiden effort.

Yetsook's lengthy training regimen wasn't for us though, and shortly thereafter we parted ways, sending our five horses, plus three others, to our original trainer, Dale Capuano. It was good to be home.

To be fair, Yetsook, somewhat gruff and abrasive, did all he could for the horses. He and his wife, Sylvia, treated them like the children they didn't have, and that is perhaps the main reason we kept him as long as we did. It cost us an estimated $49,000 over budget before we pulled the plug.

As the year 2006 dawned, we tried yet one more Charles Town trainer, Marion (Lyn) Cuttino, sending him a decent 4-year-old gelding, Pay Your Taxes, with the promise of more to follow if he were a better fit than the previous local conditioners.

JOCKEYS

Well could he ride, and often men would say
"That horse his mettle from his rider takes."

- SHAKESPEARE, *A Lover's Complaint*

Does a jockey make the difference?

I get asked that question more than one might imagine by people who think that the horse is the all-important factor in a race.

My answer is the same one I give my wife when she asks me when I'm going to mow the lawn.

"That depends."

True, the best of jockeys can't win on a slow horse, but they can, and do, make the difference between win and place when there is less than half a length between contenders.

I've seen it happen up close and personal many times. Thanks to Dale Capuano's reputation as a top trainer we had the call on many leading jockeys during our startup period. And still do.

Their names read something like a Who's Who. Kent Desmormeaux, Edgar Prado, Mark Johnston, Donald Miller, Mike Luzzi, Joe Rocco. Together they carried the Hampshire to 36 wins in its first three years (65% on the board).

Desmormeaux got the Hampshire off to a fast start. We were too green to realize it immediately but it soon became apparent that the apprentice jockey who was riding our horses regularly was special.

Only beginning his apprenticeship, this young man was winning a lot of his local races on a lot of unlikely horses, some of them ours.

"He makes a difference," was the saying that went around the track. Poor horses looked good and good horses looked excellent and excellent horses were beating the competition by a country mile.

Intrigued, I discovered that Desormeaux had started riding at age 6, clutching the mane of a tiny Shetland pony as he raced around the dirt track built by his father, Harris, in Maurice, Louisiana.

We had the call on young Kent for almost two years, by which time he had won the Eclipse Award for the best apprentice jockey in America, the first of his three Eclipses.

A few years later, he became the world's all-time one-year winningest, bypassing Chris McCarron's 586 victories with 598 wins, a record that still stands.

Desmoreaux was inducted into thoroughbred racing's Hall of Fame in 2004, after winning 4,400 races and earning almost $170 million in purses. He had also won the 1998 Kentucky Derby and Preakness on Real Quiet and the 2000 Derby on Fusaichi Pegasus. It was nice to be able to say we had the call on him way back when.

*Apprentice Kent Desormeaux poses with 5-year-old Malcolm
Barr, Jr., in Maryland, 1989.*

For a time, Desormeaux lost his way, by 1996 dropping to
the bottom of the jockey standings in his then-home base of
Southern California. As he was to readily admit, it was his own
fault. A swollen ego led him to ignore trainers' instructions,
grow lazy and arrogant, and rack up fines and suspensions for
failing to give his best efforts on every horse.

Trainer Bob Baffert helped resuscitate Desmoreaux's career
by making him vow to toe the line and putting him aboard
Real Quiet. Kent is again the jockey we knew, a polite, obliging
gentleman one can enjoy and respect. I treasure a photograph
of him with my son, who was 5 at the time, before Kent found
the big leagues in California. I was able to say hello during a
visit to Del Mar in 2005.

Edgar Prado led all North American riders in wins in both
1997 and 1998 and was a runner-up for outstanding jockey in
the 2004 Eclipse Awards.

His main claim to fame, before winning the Kentucky Derby aboard Barbaro in 2006, probably came in June, 2004, when he rode the 36-1 long shot Birdstone to a stunning victory over Smarty Jones in the Belmont, denying Smarty the Triple Crown. Smarty was a 1-5 favorite who had never lost a race.

Hampshire president Malcolm Barr, Sr. 73, with national champion jockey Edgar Prado, This photograph was taken Preakness Day, May 17, 2006, just two hours before Derby winner Barbaro broke down. Prado rode horses throughout the 1990s for the Hampshire.
Photo by Jim McCue.

I personally remember Prado best for supporting me in an English as a second language course I once taught at a local middle school. As a prize, I asked Edgar if I could bring one of my 11-year-old Hispanic students to meet him. The jockey provided the boy with a thrilling experience he'll always cherish.

Winner of the 1990 Eclipse as outstanding apprentice, Mark Johnston captured at least one Maryland Million event annually through 1994-97, and was the rider early in the career of Victory Gallop, who went on to win the 1998 Belmont Stakes.

Donald Miller, a leading Maryland jockey, rode in almost 20,000 races in his 16-year career, three of them Triple Crown races. He was the nation's leading apprentice jockey in 1981 and won the 1983 Preakness aboard Deputed Testamony. Donnie rode Probably The One for the Hampshire several times, and posed for a picture with one of our partners, Bill Verity, the former U.S. Secretary of Commerce.

Retired from racing, he is now national sales director for real estate auction specialists, Express Auction.

Mike Luzzi earned an Eclipse as the nation's leading apprentice in 1989, and, in 1993, leading all Maryland riders with 20 stakes victories, he finished second to Edgar Prado in total wins with 230.

Joe Rocco, one of our other "Who's Who" riders, still active in his late 40s, also racked up impressive wins and served as a technical advisor, along with Chris McCarron and trainer Rusty Hendrickson, on the hit movie "Seabiscuit."

Capuano must also be given credit for Ryan Fogelsonger's role in catapulting the Hampshire to national prominence by winning the $48,000 National Claiming Crown "Express" in 2003.

Fogelsonger, who had never ridden before graduating high school, got his start as an exercise boy for Capuano, and Capuano gave the 2002 Eclipse winner many of his first mounts.

Non-race fans might remember Fogelsonger from his starring role in a MTV reality show "TRUE LIFE: I WANT THE PERFECT BODY."

Another jockey who we've had riding for us for many years is one of Charles Town's "winningest" and most talented - Travis Dunkelberger. Travis is another who Capuano gave an early career boost. Travis also received an early hand from our breeder friend, Randy Funkhouser.

After 17 years running the Hampshire, I've become a big, big fan of jockeys. They've chosen a career that consumes their lives and they risk serious injury or death in every race they enter.

I love to eat and can hardly imagine the discipline of someone who has to watch his weight throughout his working career.

In his first year, an apprentice jockey shouldn't exceed 105 pounds, and for the first six months, maybe only 102. Most journeymen riders can't exceed 113 pounds depending on where they are riding (in a few states they can get away with a pound or two heavier). That's it - for as long as they ride.

Jockeys can also be shortchanged when it comes to a formal education. Now, most riders start at 16 to 17 years old, which means they usually haven't graduated high school, and that can come back to haunt them.

What if after a few years they obviously aren't going to be successful? Or what if they are badly injured?

By one comparison, professional football is a sissy game, in that an injured player at least has a college education to fall back on.

A jockey's career can go from "Life is good!" to "What am I going to do?" in the twinkling of an eye.

Joe Rocco's son, Joe, Jr., underscored the danger jockeys face in every race when his career was almost ended by a July, 2004 mishap at Colonial Downs.

Young Joe suffered multiple injuries - five fractured vertebrae, two fractured ribs, a partially punctured lung, air in his abdomen and blood on his brain - as Ace's Valentine somersaulted over Ryan Fogelsonger's Come to Cashel in the upper stretch. He endured a long, painful recovery and didn't saddle up again for more than four months.

Fogelsonger escaped with a concussion and bruises. Come to Cashel had to be euthanized.

Mike Luzzi also had a couple of close calls. In 2001, he broke an ankle when Gold N Fancy flipped in the starting gate at Belmont, and he was out for the 2004 season after suffering a broken leg when thrown from Honey Fritters at Saratoga.

Joe Rocco, Jr. once had this to say about the danger jockeys face: "When you ride, you don't think about getting hurt. You can't. The day you're scared is the day you've got to quit."

14
UNSUNG HEROES

Heroes are bred by lands where livelihood comes hard.

- MEANDER, *Anephioi. Frag. 63.*

As it happens, I truly love racetracks, the Charles Town one included, and take particular pleasure in my entrée to training facilities. There isn't anything quite so enjoyable as an early morning visit to the stables. It is a wonderful experience and well worth abandoning a warm bed. As busy as he is running a major hotel in Shepherdstown, WV, one of our partners, Ken Lowe, Jr., spends many an early morning catching the early morning activity at the Charles Town track.

Watching the workouts as dawn breaks, the snorting animals pounding around the training track, mist swirling around them on a crisp autumn morning, is exhilarating indeed - and made more so by your shared ownership of the horse being conditioned. It gives the sport an extra dimension almost beyond description.

You hold your breath as the stopwatch is released, crane to see the time of the workout, and grin with pleasure when a good one is recorded. Your heart will jump a bit if the horse gets even a little bit fractious. You're afraid he'll hurt himself.

I don't go as frequently as I would wish because it is easy to get emotionally involved when too close to a horse. Many of our animals don't stay with us very long, being claimers. They move through constantly, perhaps staying only a few weeks, or maybe two to three months.

It is even more wrenching with the horses we breed. They are with us for three to four years and sometimes longer. Then most move on.

Fortunately, we manage to keep a few close by, as we did with Probably's Devil, who found a new home on a nearby farm owned by Marie Draus. Similarly, his mother, Probably The One, was adopted by her groom, Amy Nicol, and lived out her life on the Nicol farm in upstate New York. Mingling with the stable hands can be just as rewarding as visiting your horses. I have to pay high tribute to the low-paid grooms, exercise riders and hot walkers who condition these expensive, highly sensitive and delicate animals.

Probably's Devil -- he got us to Saratoga!

A breed apart, some don't fit well in open society, and are not overly communicative, which is perhaps why they work where they work. While underpaid and often carrying heavy psychological baggage, these hardworking folk are at home in the barns and able to communicate with animals with ease, if not able to relate easily to their own kind.

Of all people, big and small, that I've been acquainted with in this world, I truly rank stable hands as some of the best. Once you get to know them, and they you, they are sincere, unselfish, kind folk, some with a philosophy of life that we mainstreamers would do well to emulate. They give a lot of themselves to the horses and mostly appear to live by the Golden Rule.

Many of them have wrestled with substance abuse problems at some time in their lives. One of our former partners, Joe Fonti, has labored mostly unrecognized among backstretch workers at the Maryland tracks, counseling them on drugs and alcohol.

(Capuano won't tolerate alcohol or drug use among his employees. He'll summarily fire them for use around his stable area. However he will work with them in their rehabilitation.)

I make a special effort to visit stable workers on Thanksgiving and Christmas. In Maryland, many live like gypsies in pretty wretched conditions in the backstretch dormitories (although conditions have improved in recent years) and have little opportunity to enjoy the holiday spirit. More than most, they appreciate being remembered on the holidays, be it with some cash or perhaps a sweater or windbreaker.

I was touched one year when Erlene, who had spent extra time with the ornery R.T. Rise N Shine, helping to make him the Hampshire's clown prince, a kinder, happier and gentler animal, rewarded me with a gift of her own.

Erlene plucked, from a hiding place in R.T.'s stall, a lovely, hand-painted Christmas tree ornament. She had reproduced the hot pink and black diamonds of our jockey silks on the small glass globe, a job she had undertaken with great skill and obvious affection for me and my then young son. Her work of art is reproduced on the cover of this book.

*Erline shows off one of the Hampshire horses
to a group of admirers in March 1991.*

Apart from holiday gifts, I make it a point, after a winning race, to give a cash bonus to the horse's groom. It's not all that much, but since the most any grooms and other stable hands earn is about $400 a week, they are very pleased to get it.

Needless to say, I'm up front about what motivates this "largesse", in that it recognizes the special relationship they share with our horse. Without their careful attention many of our animals would not perform as well.

The relationships I've established with stable workers has paid dividends for the Hampshire. Partners and their friends and children are warmly received when they show up on weekend mornings with bags of carrots and mints for the horses.

Without prompting, grooms offer extra little services, taking horses out for photographs and "prettying them up" with a brush prior to the snapshot. Sometimes we are encouraged to walk the horse (if it was a particularly docile animal) and this delights our partners - and ourselves.

Grooms are never more excited than when we bring newspaper reporters and photographers into the barn area. Though invariably razzed by their colleagues, they stand proud with their horses for photographs, and look forward to publication day almost as much as we do.

I know they appreciate the fact that we try to shine the spotlight on them and the horses as well as on ourselves and the trainer.

As I've said, it is sometimes difficult to communicate with our grooms, as many of them, as is common in the industry, have limited English. But there are occasions when the gulf is readily breached.

After Landler's momentous victory, Don and Shirley Morris treated about a dozen fellow owners to dinner at a casino restaurant. I joined them along with Capuano, jockey Fogelsonger, and Landler's Hispanic groom, Abel. We noted in the restaurant that Abel had achieved absolute mastery over two words - "top sirloin".

After dinner, I hit the $5 blackjack tables with Fogelsonger and Abel. Abel, a blackjack novice whose hand I played, picked up $70, acquiring another English word, "Holy ****!", while Fogelsonger consistently lost. I heard later that Fogelsonger, who I'd given some tips on playing the game, won at Las Vegas, giving me some of the credit.

Quite apart from visiting the backstretch, the main lure of the racetrack, of course, is watching the race itself. When you own even part of a horse, you make improbable 150-mile road trips to see him perform. You try to, anyway.

I'll probably never forget setting off from Washington, D.C., in a rainstorm and early evening darkness to watch Nordic Conqueror, a broken-down $5,000 number, try his luck at Charles Town in the mid-1980s. The "Conqueror" had failed on Class I race courses, and, even at Charles Town, a track for has-beens in those days, he was going to go off at 15-1. Yet hope springs eternal, right?

Traffic was backed up for miles and I was in it. The likelihood of our horse - I was in someone else's partnership then - getting even in the first three was slim. After two hours and 35 miles, I swooped on to an exit ramp, settling for a relaxing evening at the local trotting track.

Opening the paper the next morning, I saw that Nordic Conqueror had won, paying $32 to his supporters for a $2 bet. Those syndicate members who made it to Charles Town that night got half their total partnership investment back for a $20 across -the-board bet!

Which is why I remain inclined to make improbable trips to distant tracks. And it's not for the money. You just never know.

15
PARTNERS YOU LOVE AND HATE

There are manifest asses, but you, good Leech, you are a horse of another colour.

- R.H. BARHAM, *Leech of Folkstone*

In the Hampshire, partners fall into basically two main categories, appearing on the Partners You Love to Love List and the Partners You Love to Hate List. I'm going to start with the latter list - to get it off my chest.

I'm not suggesting here that we've had a whole lot of partners who qualified for The Partners You Love to Hate List. I'm just saying we've had enough to give me heartburn.

The thing is, once a partner buys a share, it's like Colin Powell told George Bush about the Iraqis, you own them. They are not going to go away. And what some of them are tossing at you is not flowers and candy.

There was a time, in our early years, that a man and woman who had one share (they weren't related, but still had bought only the one share) were such a pain in the neck that we divided them up.

Bill Joyce handled the complaints from one. I fielded the gripes of the other. It was the only way we could keep our sanity.

I'm really glad that our initial contracts made the general partners the sole decision-making authority and that now, in the corporation, the board, which includes three directors, has the final say.

We keep a tight rein (no pun intended) because you simply cannot run horses by committee. In my journalism days I've watched committees get so far out of hand they looked like a mob in a French election. I don't want that happening at the Hampshire.

But all partners do have a say in what many may consider the most important decision. When one of our mares gives birth, what should we name the foal. Everyone suggests a name, or names. The eventual name is decided by a full vote.

As I've said, our investors have been a mixed bag from various walks of life. They've ranged from weather forecaster to banker, homemaker to shoe salesman, starving artist to multimillionaire. I sometimes think the only thing they have in common is their humanity and a burning desire to be a part of thoroughbred racing.

Most of these folks, even the rich ones, come in for a minimum stake, and few expect to make a profit. They are more interested in the fun, thrills and pride that come with owning even a small portion of a thoroughbred.

It's a surprise when they win money and more likely than not they'll put it at risk again by rolling over into the next available partnership.

Mostly, our groups are made up of easygoing, easy-to-get-along-with people, but there is always someone in the crowd - and sometimes more than one - who thinks things should be done differently.

Even now, with the Hampshire's long-established success, it may be relatively easy to sell shares, but to achieve a consensus on how to run the show? That isn't going to happen.

Which brings me to my lists, starting with, to get it off my chest, the PARTNERS YOU LOVE TO HATE LIST

THE GENIUS

He, or she, knows more than the trainer, and is not indisposed to tell the trainer he's an idiot.

Actually, Dale Capuano says, a lot of horse owners, even those who are partial owners, feel this way. Second-guessing the conditioner is part of the game and it's easy to fall into the habit.

Do you sometimes disagree with the way the kindergarten teacher is handling junior?

There you go.

THE OTHER GENIUS

He, or she, knows more than the corporation president (formerly the general partner), and is not indisposed to tell him he's an even bigger idiot than the trainer.

Obviously, that's an unfair comparison. The trainer is a trainer. I used to work for the government. Before that, a news service.

If one of us is an idiot, okay, I'll be the biggest, but why be sarcastic about it?

The Science Fiction Devotee

He is against racing on off tracks in the winter because the alleged de-icing component in the loam causes the horses' hooves to disintegrate.

Sure. And would you like an introduction to Tom Cruise?

The Strategist

If we enter a horse in a 6-furlong sprint, he says it belongs in a route (over 7 furlongs).

If a horse is "on the muscle" and we run it twice in three weeks, we're running the stock into the ground.

If we send a horse to the farm for R&R, the need, and expense, is questioned.

The guy would find something wrong with Pamela Anderson.

The Bluffers

They constantly denigrate what they call our "cheap" stock. They say they'll only be back when we get more distinguished thoroughbreds.

So we call their bluff with a high-flying endeavor that provokes some interest in the Wall Street crowd.

They decline to invest. We thank heaven.

The Cigar Crowder

He enters the winner's circle with a lighted cigar in his mouth and shoves up next to the heavily breathing animal.

The horse is spooked. The camera flashes. The horse backs off. The partners are in the picture. The horse almost isn't.

THE SAY-CHEESE DISREGARDER

He's not ready and looking the wrong way when his picture is taken in the winner's circle.

He sends the photograph back implying he's too embarrassed to hang it on his wall.

He demands his money back. We give it to him.

We're also embarrassed. The Cigar Crowder and The Say Cheese Disregarder are the same guy.

Okay, now we feel better, so here is our PARTNERS YOU LOVE TO LOVE LIST

THE TRACK IS THE BEST MEDICINE BELIEVER

The partner, like many, is retired, he has limited funds, his wife is ill with cancer, and medical expenses are piling up.

Despite the mounting bills he opts to keep his syndicate membership alive because the wife so looks forward to "their" horse's performance.

Mostly, she keeps check on the hotline, but occasionally makes it to the track. They both feel the expense is more than worthwhile.

In our opinion, they are the ones who are worthwhile, and we make an extra effort on their behalf, joining other partners in pulling for her cure and rehabilitation.

THE BURNED IN OUR MEMORY OLD MAN

He is a cheerful joy-to-have-around type who joins us early in Hampshire I. He has a lifelong ambition. It's to have his picture taken in the winner's circle with "his" horse.

His health begins to deteriorate. Now he tells he us he wants something else. Make sure, if he dies, that his share is turned over to his next-of-kin.

Happily, he gets his first wish, his picture taken in the winner's circle and when the partnership is dissolved he goes his way. We don't know where. But he made a lasting impression.

Three years later, when we're in our seventh partnership, Hampshire Curragh, Bill Joyce is caught talking to himself at the races.

"I wonder what happened to old … "

THE TRY, TRY AGAIN KID

The young government worker's name is Ken Lake. He's one of the most enthusiastic race fans you'll ever meet. His overriding dream - like the old man's - is to get his picture taken in the winner's circle.

When he attends a race, his horse , Intoxicated, is beaten. When he doesn't get to the track, Intoxicated wins.

On two occasions Ken follows Intoxicated all the way to Philadelphia. Zip.

We start wondering if we should pay the guy to stay home. Ken misses two races in a row. Intoxicated wins both of them,

THE LET'S TAKE THE MONEY AND RUN GUY

Millionaire Bill Verity retrieves his money from a Hampshire partnership because he wants to be able to say he made money on a racing venture.

The horses he owned either privately or in syndicates never made it to the winner's circle.

The Hampshire produced a winner for him - Probably The One.

THE BELLHOP WITH A HEART OF GOLD

This ex-boxer quickly loses his initial stake in the Foolish World syndicate and can't cobble together enough money to get back into the Hampshire.

The reason: he's given up some of his time on the job to an unemployed bellhop who needs the work to feed his wife and kids.

We contemplate donating a share to the Good Samaritan but finally decide it wouldn't be fair to our partners or appropriate in our high-risk business where every dollar counts. But we keep Leo Clark in the family by leaving him on our newsletter mailing list and inviting him to Hampshire-sponsored events for years after.

THE LAWYER WHO CAN SEE BOTH SIDES OF AN ARGUMENT

Dave Prestemon, a great student of horses, the kind of man who probably would spend his life at the track given independent wealth and perhaps fewer children, can't resist second-guessing new acquisitions.

He often provides computer printouts on our new claims and is sometimes critical in his observations. Yet he is invariably ready to accept the trainer's advice and await results. Mostly, he agrees, the trainer is correct.

THE LAWYER WHOSE LOVE BLOSSOMED AT THE TRACK

Richard Popkin, his brother, Ed, and Richard's son, Marshall, get huge enjoyment out of being a part of the Hampshire. They visit the horses regularly in the barns, choose favorites, regard them as pets.

Richard meets Karol and begins bringing her out to the stables. We watch with pleasure as their relationship develops and wedding bells ring. We fete them to a surprise champagne breakfast in the groom's canteen.

You may not think Karol's visits to the horses had anything to do with Cupid, but vuz you there, Charlie?

THE DARING ADVANCE PLACEMENT

In his mid-70s, Tim Gibson is like many of our more elderly, retired partners. They aren't too quick on their feet anymore and sometimes unable to walk very far.

Tim is really, really anxious to have his picture taken in the winner's circle. As we've done for other older partners, we drive him to the track on a day where there is a good chance his horse will win.

Then, full of angst, we get him positioned near the winner's circle *before* the race is run.

This is heresy in superstition-ridden horseracing. What if we have jinxed the horse?

We haven't. Tim's horse comes in first. Tim gets his picture taken in the winner's circle.

THE CHRISTMAS PRESENT SHOPPER

Eileen Buckley makes a clandestine call to the Hampshire hotline. She wants to buy her husband, Gary, a special

Christmas present - a share in a Charles Town claiming partnership.

The deal is made. Gary gets a share of Little Miss Hurry.

I'm there when Eileen and Gary show up at the track. Eileen tells him. "See that filly? She's your horse, Gary. Merry Christmas!"

Little Miss Hurry doesn't win, but the look on Gary's face tells us Eileen hit the jackpot with her unique gift.

THE BLIND MAN WHO SEEMS TO SEE

Don Morris, in his sixties and blind since his mid-40s, is an inveterate owner and race-goer who truly appears to "see" every race he attends with his lovely wife, Shirley. His other senses compensate.

It's a pleasure to watch this couple at the track and when they visit their Hampshire horses at their stalls. They are always good and generous company. It was Don and Shirley who treated about a dozen other partners to dinner after Landler's big win at Canterbury.

ALL THOSE (NON-COMPLAINERS) WHO STAY HOME

A number of our partners, for whatever reason, rarely get to the track. They follow their horses through the newspapers, through their computers, through our Hampshire Hotline. We receive their checks on time, we never hear a complaint, and occasionally we get a thank you card praising us for a job well done. We love you all!

16
YOUR NAME IN THE PAPER

Great is Journalism. Is not every able Editor a Ruler of the World, being a persuader of it?

- CARLYLE, *The French Revolution*

I doubt if Scooter Libby buys the old saw about any publicity being good publicity, but there is more than a kernel of truth in it, especially as experienced by the Hampshire. We can't lose - even when they are having fun at our expense.

We weren't long into the first partnership when a local daily, the *Prince George's Journal*, having heard about us winning our first four starts, decided to check us out.

I was delighted as the *Journal* is a county newspaper covering both Laurel and Bowie racetracks in Southern Maryland.

Joe Volz, declining to take us seriously (as did several reporters during our early days), wrote a tongue-in-cheek piece headlined BUY A RACEHORSE? NEIGH, THANKS.

Volz's article nevertheless did a good job of explaining how the Hampshire functioned and it brought us as much attention as our initial partnership's four straight victories.

Calls from racing fans increased. Did we actually launch our venture on a shoestring? Was it really true you didn't have to be a millionaire to own your own racehorse?

The response was such that we decided to open a second partnership and Volz, a freelance writer, took to writing about us seriously for the Copley News Service.

This "good press" - whether it came naturally due to our success or was self-generated by skillful public relations - was soon appearing in general newspapers as well as industry publications. We no longer had to rely on costly advertising to drum up shareholder interest.

It was all grist and here is a sampling.

Headline in Baltimore's now defunct *The Business Times*: AND THEY'RE OFF ... HAMPSHIRE RACING PARTNERSHIP OPENS THE GATES FOR TWO BUREAUCRATS TO PUSH PONIES AND PAPER

Writer Susan Kellam handed us a terrific plug: "Hampshire is on its way to developing a track record and proving that it has horse sense."

This exposure in a highly respected business journal gave us the credibility it may otherwise have taken years to earn. We received numerous inquiries.

Needless to say, *The Business Times'* four-column photograph of me, Bill Joyce and Super Operator (the horse is chomping on Bill's jacket) still hangs proudly in the Barr guest powder room.

Headline in the national newsweekly *Thoroughbred Times*: SYNDICATES DEMOCRATIZE HORSE OWNERSHIP. MARYLAND-BASED HAMPSHIRE RACING STABLE CATERS TO THE MIDDLE-CLASS OWNER.

Marty McGee, later to become one of the classier writers at the *Daily Racing Form*, gave us a lengthy and wonderful boost, reporting on how, for a token investment of upfront cash, it is relatively simple to own your own horse if you go the Hampshire route.

Our small buy-in was compared to $40,000 investments for 5% shares in large national syndicates. I got the opportunity to advance my argument that bread-and-butter stables like the Hampshire are the backbone of thoroughbred racing in America.

Later, again in the *Thoroughbred Times*, an article placed the Hampshire alongside multimillion dollar partnerships such as Centennial Farms, Team Valor and Dogwood Stable and touted us as a "low-cost alternative" to the better known and more expensive groups.

New York stock broker and Hampshire partner Michael Chorna was quoted as saying: "I can have as much fun for $3,500 as they (partners in the larger groups) can have for $35,000."

Headline in the *Washington Times*: VIRGINIA FIRM DOESN'T HORSE AROUND WHEN IT COMES TO THE RACETRACK

Key sentence: "(Barr and Joyce) have come up with a way for ordinary people to invest in the excitement - and possible profitability - of thoroughbred racing, without spending a king's ransom to do so."

Headline in the *Richmond Times-Dispatch*: WINNER'S CIRCLE. RACEHORSES OFFER 'THRILL OF A LIFETIME' FOR OWNER-PARTNERS.

It came with an across-the-page photograph of our 5-year-old gelding Splashdown winning by two lengths at Colonial Downs. This was coupled with a large photo of me screaming wildly in the stands.

The story couldn't have been more positive and my phone rang all evening with calls from potential investors. Take my money, please!

Headline in the Department of Commerce's internal newspaper *Commerce People*: DUKE TOBY MAKES PARTNERS KING FOR A DAY

The full-page story and accompanying photo was as beneficial as articles in the public media. Fellow employees make great partners.

Later, again in the 33,000-circulation *Commerce People*, there was a full-page story with photograph headlined HORSES AS A HOBBY GETS SOME COMMERCE PEOPLE OUT TO THE RACES.

This time I wrote it. I have no shame in self-promotion when it comes to the Hampshire.

(Now it can be told! For a while, half a dozen of us Commerce types were slipping out to nearby Laurel Park to catch a midweek race when we should have been hard at work. A half hour there, two minutes to watch the race, a half hour back. Scarcely anyone missed us.)

Headline in the *Thoroughbred Times*: GRASS-ROOTS EFFORTS GIVE RACING NEEDED BOOST

This article said the Hampshire and a small mid-Atlantic based fan club, the Railsitters, were, in many ways, to local thoroughbred racing what the National Thoroughbred Racing Association (NTRA) was to the sport on a national scale.

I recounted the Hampshire's success in forming low-cost partnerships and was able to advance a firmly held conviction: "Racing is run by an old boys' network. We have to get people in there who can give it a whole new look."

Headline in the *Minneapolis Star Tribune*: BLUE COLLAR PARTNERSHIP EARNS VICTORY WITH LANDLER

This was the story that equated Hampshire partners with the owners of Funny Cide, the 2003 Kentucky Derby and Preakness winner.

It said our partners almost jumped out of the balcony when Landler flashed to victory. That's true.

At about this time, I was actively courting the media. The stories heralded our move to Front Royal and sparked a new wave of interest in the Hampshire.

Headline in *The Shenandoah Valley (Virginia) Herald*: HAMPSHIRE ALLIANCE TAKES OFF

Key sentence: "The Hampshire Alliance, Inc. currently has so many partners, it will not be taking any more for the time being."

Headline in the *Quad-State Business Journal*: PARTNER-SHIPS INVEST IN SPORT OF KINGS

This lengthy article reported on the Hampshire's purchase of three thoroughbreds from Randy Funkhouser's O'Sullivan Farms in Charles Town. The $62,000 deal was fully subscribed.

Headline in the *Mid-Atlantic Thoroughbred*: MALCOLM IN THE MIDDLE

Key sentence: "Barr deserves credit for introducing thoroughbred ownership to more than 500 people."

Headline in the *Warren County (Virginia) Sentinel*: THE STAGE IS SET

The story depicted me (a board member of the local Wayside Theatre) as the director and the horses as the actors and suggested that racing fans keep an eye out for them at the track.

Headline for a Copley News Service story in *The Ridgeway (Pennsylvania) Record*: HORSE OF A DIFFERENT COLOR

Volz, now taking us seriously, wrote that while gerontologists are always expounding the virtue of trying something different when you retire, my choice, thoroughbred racing, was one for the books.

Headline in the *Northern Virginia Daily:* GROUP ALLOWS ACCESS TO 'SPORT OF KINGS'

Key paragraph: "His racing partnership takes the 'sport of kings' and makes it affordable and accessible to horse racing fans, ranging from attorneys to waiters ... participants literally get a piece of the action by buying ownership shares in the horses. The Hampshire's pink and black silks become their own, giving owners a vested interest from paddock to finish line.

Headline in the (Virginia) *Senior Beacon*: LIKE HORSE RACES? GO YOURSELF ONE BETTER

The lead paragraph said it all. "This is straight from the horse's mouth. You don't have to be a millionaire to own your own racehorse."

Headline in the *Warren County (Virginia) Sentinel*: HAMPSHIRE ALLIANCE OFFERS AFFORDABLE RACING PARTNERSHIPS

This story, continuing the theme, featured a photo of our gray mare, Karate Kat, who had recently won a $23,000 allowance race at Charles Town.

I admit that some of these stories came from actively working the media - suggesting coverage, providing angles, even calling in markers - but you aren't doing your job if you don't hustle the press. It gets a deluge of news releases every day. You have to be in there pitching - and making sure you stand out.

If there is one major lesson in all this, it is that you have to seize your public relations coups where you find them.

Let's say you learn that President Bill Clinton's mother, Ms. Virginia Kelley, a regular at Oaklawn Park race track in Arkansas, is going to attend the races at Laurel Park.

What should you do? Well, you don't sit on your hands.

Obviously, you should welcome her to Laurel, and that's what we did, taking out an ad in the *Daily Racing Form* on behalf of the "Hampshire Racing Stable."

Malcolm Barr, Sr., and Ms. Virginia Kelley, mother of President Bill Clinton, in the Turf Club at Laurel Park.

Then Bill Joyce, Washington lobbyist Tim Feldman and I crashed the "members only" Laurel Turf Club where I presented the president's mother with a Hampshire watch to commemorate her visit. (Sadly, Ms. Kelley died a couple of years later.)

Photographs were taken and I got to say my piece in the *Baltimore Sun*.

"We heard she might be coming out and we just wanted to have a voice and welcome her to Laurel as a friend of racing.

"Not since J. Edgar Hoover have we had a Washington personality so interested in the sport. We hear she's a two-dollar bettor and we think she epitomizes what racing is all about."

Which brings me to my favorite paranoid public relations conspiracy theory.

Remember all the hoopla back in 1985 when Coca-Cola fiddled with the drink's taste and introduced it as New Coke?

Remember all the hoopla when Coke customers vehemently demanded a return to the traditional drink and the company was obliged to bring it back renamed Coca-Cola Classic?

I know all kinds of people who are absolutely convinced that Coca-Cola had *planned* for New Coke to fail.

Maybe, maybe not. But either way, terrific p.r.

17
OTHER HORSES

Yet if man, of all the Creator planned,
His noblest work is reckoned,
Of the works of His hand, by sea or by land,
The horse may at least rank second.

- A.L. GORDON, *Hippodramania*

By virtue of being a winner and then our first dam, Probably The One was perhaps our most popular horse, but when it came to a horse that truly won our hearts, it was R.T. Rise N Shine, a.k.a. Mr. Personality.

A grandson of Secretariat and a son of Secretary of War, this loveable oaf was the clown prince of Hampshire, always good for a laugh.

R.T.'s great pleasure in life was peppermint and he didn't always ask politely. Case in point: Tim Feldman, one of our partners, later elevated to an at-large director, having given R.T. a peppermint, wasn't quick enough to offer him a second.

R.T. bit Feldman on the shoulder to demonstrate his desire and/or displeasure. Feldman had to buy a new coat.

But it was on the walk down to the paddock from the receiving barn that R.T. Rise N Shine rose to his greatest heights. Head held high, he would grin at the crowd, big yellow choppers agape, and then relieve himself before turning into the saddling enclosure. He took longer to get comfortable than any other horse at the track.

When we claimed R.T. for $5,000, in October, 1990, the big brown gelding was 7 years old and already had 74 races under his belt, so there were some hooting nay sayers in our midst and for a while it looked like they might be right.

He moped in his stall, and his trainer, Erline, couldn't cheer him up, even with her own brand of horse talk. "You silly, big booger," she'd say, and he'd seem to agree.

We couldn't figure it. Before coming to us he had been an accomplished speedster who ran in the upper allowance and lower stakes ranks. An old bowed tendon limited his performance but not his tenacity. Once, we sent him to the farm, keeping him in training and hoping a change of scenery would help his attitude. Thankfully it did.

When he came back three weeks later, batteries recharged, he won the first time out, and he proved to be a consistent competitor during the combined period of more than a year that we owned him.

Mostly we ran him for a nickel ($5,000) or $6,500, and usually he was second, third or fourth, rarely off the board, and once in a while he threw in a win.

It rarely happens, but his groom, Erline, became emotionally attached, and when he was claimed away for $5,000, it was partly for her that we claimed him back for $8,500. The other justification was a newly formed partnership that needed a reliable to horse to get it off to the races.

R.T. took the Hampshire Ascot (we had taken to naming partnerships after world-class race courses, mainly in Europe) to the winner's circle twice more for a total of four times for the Hampshire. In all, he was in the money or fourth 19 times out of 25 races.

His string ran out in February, 1992. Invariably in the money, he still couldn't win at the lowest levels of a class I track, so we sold him privately, knowing that he could win at a lesser track, and he did.

Appearing under his new colors at Penn National, he posted a first, second and third-place finish in his first three races. By this time, he'd run more than 100 races lifetime.

I was glad that his new owners were treating him properly. R.T. had an intensive dislike for the whip. He stopped when he was hit. He didn't stop in any of his first three races in Pennsylvania.

It is a rare horse that will get three wins in a row, but the filly Auto Train, one of the prettiest horses we ever owned, a dark brown 4-year-old charmer with a broad white streak running eyes to nose, managed to do that for us. And we got her on the cheap from a gypsy outfit.

It showed up at Laurel one day after running her around tracks in Pennsylvania and New Jersey with scant success and despite her poor record Capuano thought she looked promising.

What did we have to lose except $5,000 - then the cheapest you could buy a horse off the track in Maryland.

So we put in our bid and I watched with a mix of awe and chagrin when she broke from the gate running greenly, grabbed a huge lead, posted some impossible early speed fractions for a race, and then, of course, lost by some 20 lengths.

Still, I remained cautiously optimistic in a report in our February 1992 Newsletter, while announcing our anguished decision to retire Probably The One.

"It's too early, we know, to begin to even dream of a successor to Probably The One (our winner of $100,000, now in foal) but we dare to mention that Auto Train, a $5,000 claim for Hampshire IV and Hampshire Newmarket, may yet fill the void.

"First time out, at a distance (7f) she's neither suited nor trained for, Auto Train shot to the lead out of the gate, maintained first place until the final yards, then succumbed to the race favorite to take second place.

"Showing this turn of speed in a 7-furlong race makes us hopeful that she's capable of winning handily at 1 1/16 miles in similar company. Similarly, she displayed the same gutsiness as her predecessor in the duel down the lane ..."

Those were prophetic words, to a point. Auto Train's future races were lengthened to 8 ½ furlongs and she thrived on the distance, posting those rare three wins in a row, even though time-wise she was one of the slowest pokes we ever owned. It should be noted that it took the Hampshire three years to achieve that hat trick.

Her first two wins were by a combined total of 18 lengths at the $5,000 and $8,500 claiming levels. Her third win was a made-in-heaven outing for Auto Train, an $18,000 allowance race with conditions that allowed no other horses except those she had already competed against, and had beaten soundly.

Similar older fillies and mares were going on the grass that day and she was on the dirt track, so the major competition was siphoned off, leaving Auto Train in a short field of six. She was sent off the favorite and didn't disappoint her many supporters.

A born front runner, she shook off a couple of challengers and prevailed by half a length. However, sobriety, and mixed emotions, set in as we noted her time. It was her fastest yet. But it was nevertheless a slow 1:47.4.

For the moment, our petite, gentle $5,000 purchase had won a quick $20,000 in purses, and now it was going to be tough slogging. Finding races Auto Train could win tested Capuano's capabilities to the fullest.

Even though she had a flawless front-running style and was magnificently shepherded around the track by jockey Edgar Prado, there was no denying she was slow, and she was also difficult to spot, or find races for.

Prado would have her leap out of the gate to a big lead, then rein her in enough so that she'd have something left at the finish. Mostly, this worked, and we were to enjoy the fruits of Auto Train for several months as Capuano strove mightily to find races to fit her in, both in and out of town.

In view of her substandard times, there was no interest in claiming her, but we knew she was sound and had only to be patient to reap more profits.

Unfortunately, in September, 1992, we decided to take her to Delaware Park for a change of scenery and the chance at a small, perhaps easy, purse, and fate decreed that we leave her there. She ran a game second and was claimed by a local horseman for the $5,000 tag.

It was a sad day for everyone. Our groom, Lisa, who had also groomed Probably The One for a while, had taken a quick personal interest in her, as she was as easy to care for. The gentle filly also had been a favorite of the children who came by for photographs and to ply her with carrots and candy.

Auto Train's impressive record during her 9-month stay with us:

Races	Won	Place	Show	Fourth	Earnings
15	4	4	1	2	$29,580

Alamance County, a 3-year-old brown gelding, grandson of Triple Crown winner Secretariat, came to us in August, 1992 with a $16,000 claiming tag.

His two second-place finishes at 6 furlongs provided some excitement that fall but we frankly expected more. Then Prado recommended adding another furlong.

Much to everyone's delight, Alamance County won a $25,000 claiming race at 7 furlongs, then a conditioned allowance, helping the Hampshire compile a year-end record of 20% win 71% on-the-board for 1992.

The breakdown:

Races	Won	Place	Show	Fourth
41	8	6	8	7

Since our inception, we've informally kept our statistics this way, since fourth-place horses do, in fact, keep us technically "on-the-board" and give an indication of our horses' competitiveness.

We should note that the length of time we kept Probably The One, R.T. Rise and Shine and Alamance County in our stats was an aberration. Claiming horses normally turn over within a month or two.

18

INVOLVED PARTNERS

There where the course is,
Delight makes all of the one mind,
The riders upon the galloping horses,
The crowd that closes in behind...

- Yeats, "At Galway Races"

A successful racing syndicate is something like a successful marriage. Ann Landers would probably tell you the same thing. You must keep the lines of communication open, you also have to do the special little things (and sometimes not so little) that let the other party know you care.

As I've said, when Bill and I started out, the "communicator" job fell to me, on account of my background in journalism and public relations.

I was happy to have it, as I like to think I'm a people person. Just ask my wife.

When we married in 1983, Carol got to pick our honeymoon venue. She chose Brazil. Upon arrival in Rio de Janeiro in 105-plus temperatures after a long flight, we checked into our hotel, and while she showered I leafed through the local telephone directory and found who I was looking for - easy to spot in a Portuguese book, the name George Hawrylshyn, a Ukrainian-Canadian pal from AP days who'd gone native in South America.

I called George and we were deep in conversation when Carol emerged from the shower, horror-stricken. "I chose Brazil because you never mentioned you knew anybody here…and the first person we meet on the plane is your hairdresser and now you're talking to Lord knows who on the phone!"

Like Carol discovered early, I'm a people person. I like people; I collect people. There are few places I travel that I don't know someone close by. And, as luck would have it, George of the unpronounceable last name saved our honeymoon trip from disaster by rescuing us from our un-air conditioned room on Ipanema Beach and hosting us in his cool mountainside home 50 miles south of Rio.

My most effective tool communicating with our partners has been our round-the-clock telephone answering service, the Hampshire Hotline, 540-636-1543.

The hotline was initially installed to take calls from people responding to our first partnership's share-offer advertisements in the *Daily Racing Form*.

Soon it morphed into an easy way to keep partners informed of the syndicate's ongoing activities.

When they call the hotline, they get advance notices of races, the results of races already run, and information on off-track events such as meetings and social activities.

The hotline also provides notice of significant workouts scheduled for our horses and updates on the health of animals that may be laid up at one of the farms due to injury or illness.

To supplement the hotline, we distribute a monthly newsletter called - nothing fancy - the Hampshire Alliance, Inc. NEWSLETTER.

The bright pink four-page newsletter fills the gaps left by the brief news items on the hotline and may feature a special article by a partner or an opinion piece from my word processor. Our partners look forward to it eagerly (or so some of them tell me) and several reporters who have written about our syndicates have given it high marks.

On more than one occasion the newsletter has rallied the troops in time of need. Hampshire partners contributed generously when jockey Shannon Campbell, badly injured in a track mishap, wasn't adequately covered by insurance. Also, they helped farm manager Marie Draus pay the large vet bills incurred by one of our former homebreds, Probably's Devil, seriously hurt in a farm accident. Campbell is confined in a wheel chair. Probably's Devil, adopted by Draus when his racing career ended, fully recovered to enjoy retirement at Stonewall Farm.

At my age, into my seventies as this book is written, I've been slow to embrace the computer, but the hotline and newsletter seem to adequately serve our partners, many of whom, after all, are eligible for AARP membership.

I have to confess I'm only now starting to realize and employ e-mail's potential and as my address list grows in size to use it is becoming as important as the hotline and the newsletter.

We are gradually recruiting younger partners, 30 and 40-somethings, our "Young Turks," and they have their own representative on our board, Washington lobbyist Jim Dornan.

When appropriate, we're not averse to adding the touch of class that Kathryn Joyce used to seek for the Hampshire. Our annual meetings continue to be held at luncheons in the historic National Press Club in Washington, D.C.

We average 30 to 40 partners and guests and our featured speakers come with inside insights on the thoroughbred racing industry. For example, we've heard from breeders Michael and Josh Pons of Country Life Farm in Maryland, breeder Randy Funkhouser of O'Sullivan Farms in West Virginia, and Olive Cooney, president of the Railsitters' Fan Club. Travis Dunkelberger was the first jockey to attend one of our annual meetings in 2005.

Now for the little (and not so little) things that contribute to a successful syndicate. They come under the heading of going to the track as a group, winner's circle photographs, visits to the barns, picnics at the farms, and off-track activities that are not directly connected to the syndicate but are a lot of fun.

Beating the drum on the hotline and via the newsletter helps bump up attendance when our horses run. It is not unusual for a dozen or so partners to join me at the track when a Hampshire horse is entered. That's when we're geared for our biggest thrills but also when the biggest disappointments can occur.

When I'm at the track, which is on most all of our racing dates, I make myself useful by taking care of free admissions, partnership seating, visits to the paddock for the saddling ceremony, and brief chats with trainers and jockeys.

At both Laurel and Pimlico, we have cultivated a cordial relationship over the years with Freddie Tallarico, the venerable chief steward, who is gracious in his greeting and seating of partners and in escorting them to the winner's enclosure.

We also think highly of regular track photographers Jim McCue (Maryland) and Mike Montgomery (West Virginia) who have contributed photographs to this book and upon whom we depend so heavily for quick and efficient service. Once Mike drove 70 miles round trip to get our winner's circle photos to us on time, and Jim began an express mail service after we moved 100 miles from the Maryland tracks. Thanks, guys!

For fourteen consecutive years, we've had our own box at the Preakness, middle jewel of the Triple Crown, at which most of the crowd of 100,000 dress down, rather than up, for the May event at Baltimore's seedy Pimlico Race Course. Early partner Jerry Hill, an Orlando, Florida, resident, started the tradition and bequeathed his box to the Hampshire when he left the Washington area.

I've led as many as 35 partners and guests on the annual trek that is probably the most exciting joint outing we have in the Hampshire. In 2003, however, the high point was not the triple crown race itself. Our own Landler, the first Hampshire horse to be featured on a major race program, won the second race on the Preakness under card. About 20 of us were in the winner's circle to receive the Maryland Heritage Trophy from State Labor Secretary James D. Fielder, Jr.

The Preakness trip is our major outing, but we've also taken partners - when our horses are competing - to various tracks including Atlantic City, NJ, Saratoga, NY, Colonial Downs, VA, Mountaineer Park, WV, Delaware Park, Penn National, PA, and Canterbury Park, MN.

On these trips, we sometimes furnish transportation, make hotel reservations, and offer other amenities. Bill and I have had out-of-town partners stay with us and have enjoyed the company of new friends.

Nothing would compare of course to the celebration after Landler's win at Canterbury. As the only partnership supporting a winner at the mid-west track, our partners, or "connections," were treated like kings and queens for the day by track management.

Announcers and journalists alike made comparisons to the owners of Funny Cide, that year's Kentucky Derby and Preakness winner. It was bedlam at the trophy presentation in the winner's circle. And Landler's close victory drew the biggest applause during the replays at the VIP champagne reception following the final race.Jockey Ryan Fogelsonger took a bow.

Apart from watching "their" horse win, nothing makes partners happier than having his or her photograph taken in the winner's circle. That's why for many years we placed such great emphasis on making sure they get what many considered the nicest thanks-for-the-memories keepsakes in thoroughbred racing.

One of my old Associated Press pals, the late Paul Deith, who operated his own business, Framing By Paul, in Oaklyn, NJ, mounted and framed our winner's circle photographs for us, and all of them are masterpieces. Unfortunately, the enterprise died when he did.

We visit the barns in Maryland and West Virginia maybe eight or nine times a year, timing it so the partners may watch trainer and grooms handling their horses. And of course they get to visit the horses in their stalls.

Children and grandchildren are invited and encouraged to bring peppermint candy and carrots, so they can feed the horses.

The grooms take the animals from their stalls for photo opportunities and the trainer is usually available to explain claiming strategies and training methods.

Hampshire investors are attracted in part by the mystique of horseracing and these behind-the-scenes visits let them embrace it more closely than if they were simply fans in the grandstands.

On one of our more memorable trips to the barns, the wife of the press attache at the then-Soviet Embassy in Washington allowed her hand to follow a carrot into Beach Ballerina's mouth. She escaped a nasty bite by a nanosecond and her shriek saw the horse lift all four feet off the ground in a startled jump in the stall. The close call had international incident written all over it.

Dale Capuano, our principal trainer, is available at the stables from time to time, but otherwise personal contact is not encouraged. Messages for him and our other trainers are relayed through me.

With up to 80 partners on my side, and 60 to 80 horses in Capuano's barn, for example, the trainers have plenty to do without fielding calls from Hampshire folks, even though - some of them think - they know more than the trainer. Let's face it, second guessing the trainer is part of the fun.

Our annual picnics have grown in popularity since the birth of Probably The One's first foal, Key Probability, gave us an excuse for our first summer outing to Louis and Christine Capuano's farm at Church Hill, Maryland. Ten partners and guests showed up with their picnic baskets for that one, planting the seed for another Hampshire tradition.

Since 2000, we have sometimes topped 60 to 65 guests. There were 40 including a trainer and a favorite Charles Town security staff lady, Sue Lynn, at the 2006 picnic.

The Hampshire, make that read my wife, Carol, caters these affairs, and we pick up part of the tab, the rest financed by photo sales. We have raffles and door prizes, things for the kids to do, horses and foals to visit, and usually a trainer, breeder or jockey to give a brief talk.

These mid-summer events have hop scotched among farms in Maryland, Virginia and West Virginia.

When our mares produce foals, we make trips to the farm, even during the cold, winter months. The foals are so popular that we do not confine the visits to the owning group, but open them up to all partners, encouraging their children and grandchildren to come along.

After the first couple of years, we began to add off-track activities, starting with a trip to the high-end steeple chase races at posh Middleburg, Virginia, where, "dressed to the nines," we hosted a tailgate party.

In Maryland, where the tracks' and horsemen's organizations are more socially inclined than in West Virginia, we keep our partners updated on get-togethers such as the horsemen's Christmas party, the steeple chase meet at Fair Hill, and the annual Maryland media crab feast in aid of the back stretch scholarship fund.

In 2005, we added the West Virginia Breeders' Classic pre-race dinner and ball. Meanwhile, Carol and I have attended numerous weddings and funerals…and one Bar Mitzvah.

The Hampshire has become almost as much a social club as a racing syndicate to some partners, and that makes it even more enjoyable.

CAN YOU DO IT?

They say Princes learn no art truly, but the art of horsemanship. The reason is, the brave beast is no flatterer. He will throw a Prince as soon as his groom.

- BEN JOHNSON, *Explorata: Illiteratus Princeps*

Can you succeed in copying the Hampshire's success in the thoroughbred racing industry? Can you manage a small syndicate at a profit?

A better question: Why would you want to try?

This figure, as far as I know, is purely anecdotal, but I'm told that less than 10% of investors in thoroughbred enterprises actually realize a profit.

That's as bad as the legendary 90% first-year failure rate for restaurants. I hasten to add that the latter is now being debunked as a ridiculous myth.

If true, the restaurant industry would sail off the face of the earth. The failure rate, new research suggests, is closer to 60%.

I'm going to go with that, which would let thoroughbred racing enterprises, with a minus-10% success rate, stand alone as one of the worst rat holes in the capitalist world.

I know I've argued throughout this book that a Hampshire investment is at least as good as a Wall Street fling, but that was studiously avoiding a salient fact. In the stock market, you pay your money and worry. In managing a racing syndicate, you pay your money and worry and work your rear end off.

There is a lot more to do than simply raise money, buy a horse, waltz over to the winner's circle, and share the pool when the partnership closes.

The year begins with the annual renewal of licenses, always a headache. We are licensed in six states, Maryland, Delaware, New York, Pennsylvania, Virginia and West Virginia. Despite a "multi-jurisdictional" licensing form introduced in the 1990s, each jurisdiction has its own peculiar set of rules. It is not unusual, because of some bookkeeping snafu (on their part) or a misunderstanding (on mine) for me to have to dash off to fill out yet one more form to satisfy one more regulation so our horses can legally compete or we can legally claim.

Mistakes usually come to light on a race day early in the year when you either want to enter a horse or have your eye on claiming one. That's when the dashing around begins, often to a notary public, to the state commission, to the racing secretary's office, the track bookkeeper, or some variation of that order.

Penalties are invoked against improperly licensed or unlicensed owners and winning purses can be revoked or claims invalidated. Either tends (and this is putting it mildly) to anger partners. The good news is that as the years have gone by, the routines have become less fraught.

I can't begin to estimate how many unpaid hours I've put into making the Hampshire a success. They are beyond calculation. Ask my bookkeeper wife.

Which brings us again to that better question: Why would you want to try?

And there can only be the one answer: For the fun, excitement, thrills and camaraderie of being in the racing game - and for the bragging rights that come with a victory.

So forget the money. It's truly of much, much lesser importance. If you make some, fine. If you don't, so what? You're not in it for the money.

Okay, maybe a little, but definitely not entirely, and hardly even close. Remember that 10% success rate.

But remember too that it doesn't have to be that low. The Hampshire isn't the only success story. Obviously, while many syndicates fall by the wayside, many others still manage to hold together.

The real measure is staying on top for an extended period--as much a surprise to our lead trainer, Dale Capuano, as anything else we've accomplished. But, as I said at the start, you do that by working hard, learning from your mistakes and the mistakes of others, being innovative, never losing faith, and sharing the risks as well as the rewards.

That has always been the Hampshire's credo and it has paid off for us. Seventeen years is considered a very long time in this business. Our trainers and jockeys have told us many times that they would kill for our lifetime win (21%) and on-the-board (65%) record. It has been as high as 44% win, 60% on-the-board (2002), and as abysmally low as 9% win, 69% on-the-board (1999).

Now. Close your eyes. Still interested in trying to copy the Hampshire's success?

If the answer is yes, open them wide, which is how they should stay in this business, and try to benefit from what is meant to be my honest advice if not wise counsel. I'll try to keep any repetition to a minimum.

KNOW WHAT YOU WANT TO DO

Do you intend to get into claiming? Buying at the public auctions? Purchasing young horses at the breeding farms? Or perhaps even buying your own brood mare to obtain a foal for racing?

Whatever you do, you have to focus when starting out. Trying to do even two things at once is a sure recipe for disaster.

FORGET THAT ADVICE AS SOON AS POSSIBLE

The one constant of a racing partnership, if it is to be at all successful, is change. It must be dynamic. So, as soon as you are comfortable in the saddle, start trying new things, and do so constantly.

Throughout its history, the Hampshire has been on a roller-coaster ride, and the periods when we have bottomed out were rarely pleasant.

Partners have bought into the Hampshire for fun and excitement. They are happy at the race track. They are content to see their horses run. Optimism always runs high.

Consequently, the four times out of five that their horses lose, they are bound to experience disappointment. To help them get over it - and they do, most of the time - be sure to have new irons in the fire.

To keep up the interest, try racing at different tracks, buying instead of claiming, embarking on a breeding program, hiring your first woman trainer, etc. Or do something as dramatic as flying a horse all the way to Minnesota!

Whatever you do, don't stand still.

DON'T BE INTIMIDATED BY THE MYSTIQUE

I think more people are scared off by the mystique of thoroughbred racing rather than the red tape and licensing and accounting procedures.

The latter are common to many endeavors. Try being a used car dealer without going through hell. Everyone is over-regulated these days. Including pigeon fanciers.

It would be helpful if racing managements and track offices did more to encourage new blood. It could only be to their advantage.

Until they do - and don't look for significant change any time soon - you will just have to wade in and get it done, and not let your partners worry about it.

I should add that one of the definitions of mystique is magic and there is nothing wrong with magic. Why draw back on that account?

NEVER UNDERCAPTALIZE

Hampshire investors presently pay $3,500 per share for a capitalization of $30,000 to $35,000 in a claiming partnership and about $70,000 if we plan to buy several young horses directly from a breeder.

This way, whether claiming or buying, we have sufficient money to support a horse for six months without winning a purse at whatever the daily training rate is at a track (presently, our average is $45 at Charles Town, close to $60 at Laurel or Pimlico).

Some potential partners may argue for a cheaper share or lower capitalization but it is vital to have a minimum safety net that keeps you about six months out of bankruptcy.

TRY TO AVOID SURPRISES

Investors don't like surprises. In the Hampshire, we strive to keep them to an absolute minimum.

Normally, particularly in claiming partnerships, there should be nothing for owners to pay beyond the initial capitalization charge and the $20 we assess for a winner's circle photograph.

You can manage this by careful budgeting and setting aside specific amounts for administrative costs and fees and not exceeding them.

On rare occasions, as in the case of a promising 2-year-old who required costly throat surgery and a lengthy period of recovery, we have had to go back for additional funds. In this instance, it was $500 per share. Fortunately the animal was part of a three-horse purchase and one of them turned out to be an overnight stakes prospect.

GET THE BEST POSSIBLE TRAINER

This, of course, is easier said than done, and the Hampshire was extremely fortunate to obtain Dale Capuano, due mainly to the introduction by my friend, the late Larry Lacey.

Finding an excellent trainer and staying with him is a major key to success. You should also pick a trainer who fits your specific needs.

Let's assume you are going to start out in the claiming game. If so, you need a <u>claiming trainer</u>, someone with the knack of spotting a horse's perhaps nebulous talents, be it in the paddock, in a training session, or in a race.

In my experience, this is one of those rare gifts denied ordinary mortals, and if you hire a trainer who missed out when presents were being passed around, you are not going to succeed as a claiming partnership. There is no sense trying to improve a horse if he's no good in the first place and it's not your job to pick between good and bad. You should just have to provide the money!

There are many trainers who couldn't spot a decent claiming horse if their lives, never mind their livelihoods, depended on it, and the best trainer in the world is useless if you are in the claiming business and he can't claim a decent horse on occasion.

It goes without saying that you also need a man or woman who can read a horse, readily identifying the animal's physical problems, and believe me, all horses have them, whatever their caliber.

You can save yourself a lot of trouble by following the buyer-beware rule. One Maryland-based trainer into heavy advertising has never returned a profit for the owners who have hired him. At one point his horses had won just a dozen of 300 starts in five years.

The best approach when seeking a trainer is to simply ask around. We used to begin at the racing secretary's office but they generally don't know any more than the next guy, though they have their favorites.

We got better leads talking to breeding farm owners and learning who they were using to train their young horses. And don't hesitate to approach trainers in their barns. We were nervous about it at first. You don't need to be. Trainers welcome new clients and most will make you feel comfortable.

You should also keep careful watch at the track to see who is making the most successful claims.

This is only going to cost you time - and it's time well spent.

BE THE TRAINER'S SOLE CONTACT

I have said it before but it is worth repeating. You, and only you, should maintain regular contact, a minimum of three times a week by telephone plus infrequent personal meetings.

Your trainer has enough to do without fielding a barrage of queries from partners. If someone has a legitimate question, have them go through you, not directly, and make this a hard and fast rule.

Otherwise you are inviting anarchy.

MEANWHILE, WATCH HIM LIKE A HAWK

I am not suggesting you should challenge a trainer's judgment at every turn. I am stressing that he shouldn't be given a completely a free hand.

As I've recounted, if he eats up your budgeted funds unnecessarily, the partnership is going to be in big financial trouble.

Don't allow that to happen. Pull the plug before it gets anywhere near that stage. You owe it to your partners. They are trusting you to manage the partnership judiciously.

Unfortunately, we didn't follow our instincts, and see where it got us.

Hampshire Racing Partnership(M. Barr) - Owner
Marion L. Cuttino - Trainer
O'Sullivan Farms - WV
7 Furlongs 1:29:1
PAY YOUR TAXES
Charles Town Races
Brandon Whitacre - Up
Pineapple Pete - 2nd
Hot Skor - 3rd
April 20, 2006

Learn from the name of this horse. Always, stay on the right side of Uncle Sam, file on time, and pay your taxes! Photo by Mike Montgomery.

BUY FROM ESTABLISHED FARMS

Frankly, I'd recommend going the claiming route at first, because the horse has a track record, and you can pretty much know what you're getting for a predetermined price. If, for whatever reason, you decide to buy young horses, stick to well-established enterprises.

In my neck of the woods, I've been very happy with Country Life Farm in Bel Air, the oldest breeding farm in Maryland, and, despite the training debacle, the Funkhouser family's O'Sullivan Farm in West Virginia.. They are the type of operations you should look for wherever you are located. A farm that has been breeding for an extended period and that has built up a good reputation.

Again, do your research.

THE MORE THE MERRIER

As you progress, start thinking about several horses for one partnership. As long as you budget accordingly, it can be a more interesting, and often much more exciting, way to go. Importantly, it provides the partners with action at the track.

There are those who will disagree with this approach. Randy Funkhouser is foremost among them, perhaps because the only single-horse partnership the Hampshire ever had was with O'Sullivan Farm-bred Three Aces, and he was singularly successful. An $18,000 purchase, he won $63,352 in 2005 and his owners got a good return on their invested dollars.

My own feeling is that with, say, three horses, there is a good chance one will be a winner, another might enjoy a modicum of success, and the other could be destined to fail.

If this scenario plays out, your partners will consistently have a winning horse or two to watch at the track. If you have only one horse and it's a total bust, that's it. It's over.

WHO'S THE BOSS?

You are. Legally, a small board is required to conduct business as a limited partnership, a limited liability company or a corporation, but horse racing generally doesn't lend itself to management by committee.

Advice is fine. But you need one person making the final decisions.

Too many cooks truly do spoil the broth.

COMMUNICATE, COMMUNICATE, COMMUNICATE

Nothing is more important than well-informed partners. You can't just take their money and leave them in the dark. They want to know what is happening - and rightly so.

Establish a telephone hotline, send out e-mails, publish a monthly newsletter, operate a website.

Like the Hampshire, if a partner leaves a question on the hotline, guarantee a reply within 24 hours.

Put yourself in the partner's shoes. Wouldn't you want to know the latest news?

LUKE 11:33

No man, when he hath lighted a candle, putteth it in a secret place, neither under a bushel …

Good point. Unless you have a huge raft of relatives, friends and business associates, you will have to do some advertising initially.

When you do, remember to have a hotline answering service in place, so if you're not able to answer the phone, you'll have a recorded pitch ready for people responding to your ad.

Who would be so dumb not to do that? We were (for a little while).

If you aren't a stiff at public speaking, you might consider holding an occasional sales seminar, but don't overdo it. They can be expensive and you aren't selling big-buck timeshares.

Word-of-mouth can be more effective. Keep handing out business cards and talking up the business. Encourage your partners to do the same.

The best of all worlds is the free media publicity that has worked so well for the Hampshire. Don't be shy about feeding items and story ideas to your local weekly newspaper. All it takes is a brief note or telephone call.

HUG YOUR BOOKKEEPER

Yes, any business needs a professional, or at least semi-professional, bookkeeper who they can trust. But it is doubly important in thoroughbred racing.

My wife Carol isn't just a bean counter. It's up to her to hoist an advance warning flag when a partnership is getting close to the edge. I listen to her more carefully now. (It was hard before. Wives are, well, wives.)

Knowing when to move unproductive horses off the roster is key to staying solvent. So don't necessarily wait for the trainer to start voicing doubts. Listen to your bookkeeper too.

MAKE IT A SOCIAL ACTIVITY

A racing syndicate isn't as much fun as it could be if it's all business. There's a place - and a good reason - for group outings to the track, visits to the backstretch, and annual picnics at various farms.

It's here that camaraderie abounds and friendships are forged.

You'll be surprised at how diverse groups of people can knit so closely and it certainly doesn't harm the business. Friends are more likely to want to stay together when it is time to form a new partnership.

Incidentally, when visiting the backstretch, it is a great idea to meet afterwards in the track canteen, which provides the ideal atmosphere for discussing new programs and contemplating new partnerships.

And please, please, please don't forget the value of winner's circle photographs. Providing them to our partners is perhaps the most important function we perform.

KEEP IT SIMPLE

Originally, Bill Joyce, as lawyers are wont to do, produced a 27-page legal agreement for partners to sign, but this was later replaced by a single page based on one used by a multimillion-dollar British thoroughbred partnership.

I admire its straightforward simplicity and would recommend it to anyone contemplating forming a horse racing venture similar to the Hampshire. Here is a sample:

HAMPSHIRE (MARYLAND/ DELAWARE 2005) RACING UNIT

Hampshire Alliance, Inc. (Maryland/Delaware 2005) Racing Unit Agreement

Full Name _____

Social Security No._____

Address _____

Telephone _____

e-Mail_____

1. For payment of $3,500.00 the above named obtains two (2) shares of the Hampshire (Maryland/Delaware 2005) Racing Unit. Each share is $1,750.00. After subscribing to two (2) shares, additional shares, including single shares, may be obtainable at the discretion of the Corporation.

2. The Unit, comprising owners of a minimum 20 shares (maximum 24 shares) will be administered under the rules of the Hampshire Alliance, Inc., registered as a Corporation in the state of Delaware.

3. The Unit will dissolve upon final claim, sale or disposal of the horses, in May/June, 2007. On or about that date, the Unit may be extended for 12 months after the dissolution date, at the discretion of the Corporation.

4. Upon dissolution, each share will be redeemed based on its value at the time the grouping is dissolved. Each share owner will receive tax information at the end of the duration of the Hampshire (Maryland/Delaware 2005) Racing Unit.

5. For services rendered, the Corporation will receive 5% of the proceeds of the Unit upon dissolution. The Corporation will receive seven and one half (7 ½%) per cent of gross purses, as well as five (5%) of the profits of the sale of horses, either by claim or private sale. Costs of winner's circle photographs and extracurricular events will be borne by the share owner. Reasonable administration costs will be charged to the Unit.

6. The horses shall remain the property of the Corporation and shall race in the colors (pink and black diamonds) of the Corporation. The Hampshire Alliance, Inc. shall retain all trophies and prizes, other than purses, for its archives.

7. The management, training, racing, times and methods of sale or disposal of the horses shall be the responsibility of the Corporation.

8. Each year, in December, an annual meeting will be held for all share owners of all the Hampshire Alliance, Inc. units.

_____   _____

Signature of Share Owner   Date

_____   _____

For Hampshire Alliance, Inc.   Date

FINALLY, MAKE "KILLER" YARDS OFF LIMITS

As an animal lover, I consider it sinful to send a thoroughbred horse to a slaughter house. We call it "to the killers." It takes effort, but old, injured, or just worn-out and slow horses deserve to be placed in caring homes.

The Hampshire achieves that by maintaining a trap line of farms willing to adopt or rescue these animals. Most will make someone a wonderful pet, a riding horse, or perhaps even a dressage horse or hunter. Their racing days may be over but they can still enjoy useful lives.

That's about it.

The Hampshire Alliance, or, as it is better known, the Hampshire Racing Partnerships, continues as a work in progress. At age 73, I don't know how long I will be active as its president and chief operating officer, or who, if anyone, I will hand it off to.

For the time being, blessed by good health and the optimism one must have to be involved in racing and breeding thoroughbreds, I intend to hang in there. I get great delight in watching my many partners, some young, a lot as old as myself, go just a little nuts cheering for THEIR horses. And when our pink and black silks flash first past the finish line?

There is no happier bedlam.

Let me conclude with how I've finished my Hampshire Hotline messages more than 6,400 times over the many years since Bill and I put the first partnership group together.

I'LL SEE YOU IN THE WINNER'S CIRCLE!

HAMPSHIRE RACING PARTNERSHIP

The following is a list of horses, the dates upon which they raced, and the result of that race, from the date of our first claim -- Duke Toby on December 8, 1988 -- to our last race of 2005 -- Three Aces on December 11. Three Aces won that day, and Duke Toby won his first time out on January 17, 1989. A note we made at the time was that Duke Toby's first track appearance was delayed by "bad weather." Similarly, the rest of the month of December 2005 kept three of Three Aces' stable companions out of their races because of bad weather, making him the last of 25 horses to race for us that year.

Inexplicably, we began keeping our records without recording purses (although they were all kept track of in our ledgers). Perhaps this was because in the early days, we really didn't expect to win anything very much, certainly nothing like the 120th race that Three Aces recorded for the Hampshire almost 17 years later.

We also began recording fourth places as part of our on-the-board statistics since we felt this indicated the competitiveness of our horses, even though they did not figure, for the most part, in the betting. Once in awhile, they would be part of a superfecta, for example.

1989

Jan. 17	Duke Toby	Won
Jan. 28	Duke Toby	Won, claimed
Feb. 6	Super Operator	Claimed
March 21	Super Operator	Won
April 13	Super Operator	Won
April 15	Smart Falcon	Claimed
May 6	Super Operator	Fourth
May 13	Super Operator	Fourth
May 15	Foolish World	Claimed
May 27	Smart Falcon	Third
June 4	Foolish World	Seventh
June 4	Super Operator	Eighth
June 5	Smart Falcon	Third
June 18	Smart Falcon	Won, claimed
July 8	Super Operator	Eighth, claimed
July 11	Half Hearted	Claimed
July 25	Half Hearted	Fifth, claimed
July 27	Foolish World	Seventh
Aug. 3	Summer Troll	Claimed
Aug. 13	Jima Fair	Claimed
Aug. 19	Summer Troll	Third

Aug. 23	Foolish World	Fourth
Sept. 8	Foolish World	Fifth
Sept. 15	Jima Fair	Third, claimed
Sept. 19	Summer Troll	Won
Sept. 30	Summer Troll	Fifth
Sept. 30	Foolish World	Ninth
Oct. 15	Summer Troll	Ninth, claimed
Oct. 19	Masked Hilo	Claimed
Oct. 24	Due It Smoothly	Claimed
Oct. 26	Foolish World	Sixth
Nov. 5	Due It Smoothly	Fifth
Nov. 6	Masked Hilo	Fifth, claimed
Nov. 17	Authentic Spin	Claimed
Nov. 19	Foolish World	Sold
Dec. 7	Due It Smoothly	Eighth
Dec. 9	Authentic Spin	Won
Dec. 15	Authentic Spin	Second
Dec. 26	Authentic Spin	Third
Dec. 29	Beach Ballerina	Claimed
Dec. 31	Due It Smoothly	Fifth

1990

Jan. 4	Authentic Spin	Third
Jan. 7	Beach Ballerina	Sixth
Jan. 18	Alfresco	Second
Jan. 20	Due It Smoothly	Eleventh
Jan. 23	Authentic Spin	Second
Jan. 26	Due It Smoothly	Second
Jan. 30	Beach Ballerina	Second
Feb. 2	Alfresco	Fifth
Feb. 4	Authentic Spin	Second
Feb. 11	Beach Ballerina	Won
Feb. 11	Due It Smoothly	Seventh
Feb. 11	Alfresco	Fourth
Feb. 17	Authentic Spin	Second
Feb. 23	Beach Ballerina	Second
Feb. 28	Due It Smoothly	Won
Mar. 2	Priceless Pleasures	Claimed
Mar. 5	Authentic Spin,	Seventh, claimed
Mar. 6	Alfresco	Sold
Mar. 9	Beach Ballerina	Fifth
Mar. 11	Due It Smoothly	Fifth
Mar. 11	Priceless Pleasures	Eighth

Mar. 27	Beach Ballerina	Third
Apr. 12	Arlene's Bid	Claimed
Apr. 19	Priceless Pleasures	Fourth
Apr. 28	Priceless Pleasures	Third
May 8	Priceless Pleasures	Second
May 28	Beach Ballerina	Fifth
May 29	Priceless Pleasures	Eighth, claimed
June 6	Beach Ballerina	Sixth
June 15	Beach Ballerina	Fourth
June 17	B.F. Egypt	Claimed
July 8	B.F. Egypt	Fifth
July 16	Beach Ballerina	Sold
July 19	B.F. Egypt	Third, claimed
July 29	Probably The One	Claimed
Aug. 7	French Impulse	Claimed
Aug. 26	French Impulse	Sixth
Sept. 7	French Impulse	Won, claimed
Sept. 16	Probably The One	Won
Sept. 22	French Impulse	Fifth
Sept. 23	Probably The One	Won
Oct. 11	Probably The One	Second
Oct. 14	Braude's Girl	Claimed

Oct. 25	Probably The One	Third
Oct. 27	R.T. Rise N Shine	Claimed
Nov. 15	R.T. Rise N Shine	Sixth
Nov. 17	Probably The One	Won
Nov. 30	Probably The One	Third
Dec. 1	R.T. Rise N Shine	Second

1991

Jan. 1	Arlene's Bid	Second
Jan. 20	Arlene's Bid	Fourth
Jan. 21	R.T. Rise N Shine	Second
Jan. 24	Probably The One	Won
Jan. 27	Arlene's Bid	Sixth
Jan. 28	Mighty Ken	Claimed
Jan. 31	R.T. Rise N Shine	Won
Feb. 5	Arlene's Bid	Fourth
Feb. 12	Probably The One	Won
Feb. 14	R.T. Rise N Shine	Won
Feb. 16	Arlene's Bid	Fourth
Feb. 17	Mighty Ken	Fifth
Feb. 21	Probably The One	Sixth
Feb. 28	Mighty Ken	Won

March 2	R. T. Rise N Shine	Fourth
March 2	Arlene's Bid	Fifth, claimed
March 3	Probably The One	Won
March 15	Braude's Girl	Third
March 16	R.T. Rise N Shine	Seventh
March 16	Mighty Ken	Eighth
March 19	Sweet Sybil	Claimed
Mar 22	Probably The One	Second
April 4	Mighty Ken	Eighth
April 5	Probably The One	Fourth
April 6	Braude's Girl	Second
April 7	R.T. Rise N Shine	Third
April 16	Sweet Sybil	Second
April 19	R.T. Rise N Shine	Fifth
April 27	Sweet Sybil	Won
April 30	R.T. Rise N Shine	Fourth
April 30	Dr. Cookie	Claimed
May 2	Probably The One	Won
May 9	Braude's Girl	Fifth
May 10	Sweet Sybil	Sixth
May 11	Braude's Girl	Sold
May 14	Storming Back	Claimed

May 16	Probably The One	Sixth
May 30	Sweet Sybil	Won
June 4	Probably The One	Sixth
June 14	Sweet Sybil	Fourth, claimed
June 29	R.T. Rise N Shine	Won, claimed
July 4	Sir Landseer	Sixth
July 6	Probably The One	Won
July 11	Storming Back	Fifth
July 13	R.T. Rise N Shine	Claimed
July 26	Storming Back	Fourth
July 27	All Laughter	Claimed
July 28	Probably The One	Second
Aug. 1	Storming Back	Sold
Aug . 6	R.T. Rise N Shine	Second
Sept. 1	All Laughter	Won
Sept. 14	R.T. Rise N shine	Third
Sept. 18	Blow By	Claimed
Sept. 22	All Laughter	Third
Sept. 26	R.T. Rise N Shine	Fifth
Oct. 1	Dr. Cookie	Seventh
Oct. 3	R.T. Rise N Shine	Ninth
Oct. 5	All Laughter	Third

Oct. 7	Blow By	Tenth
Oct. 11	Dr. Cookie	Seventh
Oct. 15	All Laughter	Won
Oct. 19	Blow By	Ninth
Oct. 26	Dr. Cookie	Seventh
Dec. 3	Dr. Cookie	Sold
Dec. 7	All Laughter	Broke down
Dec. 8	Blow By	Ninth
Dec. 8	R.T. Rise N Shine	Third
Dec. 20	R.T. Rise N Shine	Third
Dec. 29	Blow By	Tenth, claimed

1992

Jan. 3	R. T. Rise N. Shine	Third
Jan. 4	Probably The One	Won
Jan. 10	R.T. Rise N Shine	Won
Jan. 19	Probably The One	Fifth
Jan. 21	Auto Train	Claimed
Jan. 24	R.T. Rise N Shine	Fourth
Feb. 4	R. T. Rise N Shine	Fourth
Feb. 16	Auto Train	Second
Feb. 21	R.T. Rise N Shine	Sixth

Feb. 25	R.T. Rise N Shine	Fourth
Feb. 28	R.T. Rise N Shine	Sold
March 3	Auto Train	Fourth
March 27	Auto Train	Won
April 16	Auto Train	Won
April 26	Ride Cowboy	Claimed
April. 28	Auto Train	Won
May 9	Ride Cowboy	Third
May 23	Auto Train	Seventh
May 31	Ride Cowboy	Third, claimed
June 5	Leehawk	Claimed
June 5	Brother Roberts	Claimed
June 13	Auto Train	Third
June 19	Leehawk	Second
June 19	Brother Roberts	Fifth, claimed
June 21	Auto Train	Fourth
June 30	Federal League	Claimed
July 7	Leehawk	Eighth, claimed
July 14	Auto Train	Second
July 17	Federal League	Third, claimed
July 24	Minimarine	Claimed
Aug. 14	Minimarine	Sixth

Aug. 14	Auto Train	Tenth
Aug. 19	Auto Train	Won
Aug. 22	Minimarine	Sixth
Aug. 27	Alamance County	Claimed
Aug. 30	Auto Train	Second
Sept. 13	Alamance County	Third
Sept. 17	Auto Train	Ninth
Sept. 19	Minimarine	Twelfth
Sept. 24	Minimarine	Sold
Sept. 27	Ima Social Climber	Claimed
Oct. 3	Auto Train	Second, claimed
Oct. 6	Alamance County	Third
Oct. 13	Alamance County	Won
Oct. 16	Ima Social Climber	Third
Oct. 25	Ima Social Climber	Seventh
Oct. 27	Alamance County	Won
Nov. 11	Alamance County	Fourth
Nov. 28	Alamance County	Fourth
Dec. 5	Infrastructure	Claimed
Dec. 6	Alamance County	Sixth
Dec. 31	Alamance County	Second

1993

Jan. 1	Infrastructure	Fourth
Jan. 18	Infrastructure	Fourth
Jan. 21	Alamance County	Fifth, claimed
Jan. 31	Infrastructure	Fifth
Feb. 4	Infrastructure	Won
Feb. 15	Infrastructure	Fifth
Feb. 21	Royal Victoria	Claimed
Feb. 22	A Magic Emperor	Claimed
March 2	Royal Victoria	Second
March 5	A Magic Emperor	Won
March 11	Ima Social Climber	Fifth
March 16	Royal Victoria	Eighth
March 22	Ima Social Climber	Seventh
March 23	A Magic Emperor	Won
March 31	Ima Social Climber	Fourth
April 3	A Magic Emperor	Won, claimed
April 3	Infrastructure	Fourth
April 12	Royal Victoria	Won
April 12	Ima Social Climber	Won
April 19	Ima Social Climber	Fourth
April 27	Infrastructure	Fifth

April 29	Royal Victoria	Seventh
May 8	Infrastructure	Sixth
May 14	Ima Social Climber	Won
May 18	Ima Social Climber	Sold
May 18	Infrastructure	Sold
May 21	Royal Victoria	Fifth
May 27	Intoxicated	Fifth
June 6	Royal Victoria	Fourth, claimed
June 12	Intoxicated	Eighth
June 24	Intoxicated	Sixth
July 16	Intoxicated	Second
July 31	Intoxicated	Third
Aug. 9	Jan's Special	Purchased
Aug. 13	Intoxicated	Third
Aug. 28	Intoxicated	Won
Sept. 10	Intoxicated	Second
Sept. 11	Just A Twinkling	Claimed
Sept. 24	Intoxicated	Second
Oct. 8	Intoxicated	Second
Oct. 11	Just A Twinkling	Third
Oct. 22	Intoxicated	Seventh
Oct. 25	Jan's Special	Tenth

Nov. 5	Intoxicated	Won
Nov. 15	Just A Twinkling	Won
Nov. 16	Intoxicated	Tenth, claimed
Nov. 23	Jan's Special	Sixth
Dec. 2	Just A Twinkling	Sixth
Dec. 2	Jan's Special	Sixth
Dec. 8	Just A Twinkling	Sold
Dec. 19	Jan's Special	Won

1994

Jan. 23	Jan's Special	11th
Feb. 27	Jan's Special	6th
Mar. 8	Jan's Special	Sold
Nov. 29	Dance With Luck	Claimed
Dec. 6	Dance With Luck	Won
Dec. 30	Dance With Luck	Third

1995

Jan. 9	Dance With Luck	Second
Jan. 26	Dance With Luck	Fifth
Jan. 16	Dance With Luck	Second
March. 1	Dance With Luck	Won

March. 11	Solar Angle	Claimed
March 26	Solar Angle	Fourth
April 8	Solar Angle	Fourth
April. 25	Solar Angle	Fourth
May 5	Whenourshipcomesin	Claimed
May 18	Solar Angle	Won
June 6	Solar Angle	Third
June 8	Whenourshipcomesin	Sixth
June 20	Solar Angle	Seventh
June 24	Solar Angle	Sold
July 1	Whenourshipcomesin	Fourth
July 18	Whenourshipcomesin	Seventh
Aug. 18	**Key Probability**	**Fifth**
Sept. 14	**Key Probability**	**Ninth**
Sept. 30	Collected Light	Claimed
Oct. 5	**Key Probability**	**Fifth**
Oct. 20	Collected Light	Fifth
Oct. 26	**Key Probability**	**Third**
Nov. 6	Collected Light	Fifth
Nov. 11	**Key Probability**	**Second**
Nov. 21	**Key Probability**	**Second**
Dec. 1	Collected Light	Won, claimed

Dec. 9	**Key Probability**	**Won**
Dec. 10	Decoder	Claimed
Dec. 20	Decoder	Fifth

1996

Jan 7	Decoder	Fifth, claimed
Jan. 21	**Key Probability**	**Fifth**
March 26	Okeme Not	Claimed
April 21	Okeme Not	Won
May 4	Okeme Not	Third
May 17	Okeme Not	Sixth, claimed
May 24	Great Outdoors	Claimed
June 23	Great Outdoors	Sixth
Aug. 4	Great Outdoors	Eighth
Aug. 9	Estacado	Claimed
Aug. 30	Great Outdoors	Third
Sept. 2	Estacado	Fifth
Sept. 11	Great Outdoors	Fifth
Sept. 24	Estacado	Won
Oct. 4	Great Outdoors	Third
Oct. 11	Great Outdoors	Sold
Oct. 13	Estacado	Won
Oct. 19	Whenyourshipcomesin	Eighth

Oct. 29	Estacado	Seventh
Nov. 2	Whenyourshipcomesin	Eighth
Nov. 11	Whenyourshipcomesin	Sixth
Nov. 16	**Key Probability**	**Eighth**
Nov. 16	Whenyourshipcomesin	Sold
Nov. 24	Estacado	Won
Nov. 29	**Key Probability**	**Third**
Dec. 3	Estacado	Seventh
Dec. 14	**Key Probability**	**Seventh**
Dec. 26	Duke's Star	Sixth

1997

Jan. 2	Duke's Star	Won
Jan. 3	**Key Probability**	**Second**
Jan. 8	Estacado	Second
Jan. 12	Duke's Star	Won
Jan. 26	Duke's Star	Third
Feb. 6	Estacado	Won
Feb. 7	**Key Probability**	**Third**
Feb. 9	Duke's Star	Second
Feb. 22	Duke's Star	Fourth, claimed
Feb. 26	May Testamony	Ninth
March 1	**Key Probability**	**Seventh**

March 5	Estacado	Fifth
March 9	May Testamony	Seventh
March 26	May Testamony	Sixth
April 9	Estacado	Fifth
April 13	Estacado	Sold
May 10	**Key Probability**	**Seventh**
May 15	He's Whistlin Dixie	Claimed
May 22	**Key Probability**	**Sixth**
June 11	He's Whistlin Dixie	Ninth
June 18	**Key Probability**	**Fifth**
June 22	He's Whistlin Dixie	Sixth
July 11	He's Whistlin Dixie	Fourth
July 14	**Key Probability**	**Sold**
July 20	He's Whistlin Dixie	Retired
Aug. 27	Sly Goldust	Fourth
Sept. 10	**Probably's Halo**	**Seventh**
Sept. 10	Sly Goldust	Sixth
Oct. 1	**Probably's Halo**	**Won**
Oct. 31	Sly Goldust	Ninth
Nov. 22	**Probably's Halo**	**Fifth**
Dec. 11	Probably's Halo	Seventh

1998

Jan. 2	**Probably's Halo**	**Won**
Jan. 18	**Probably's Halo**	**Seventh**
Feb. 2	King Merlin	Claimed
Feb. 13	**Probably's Halo**	**Third**
Feb. 16	King Merlin	Fifth
Feb. 16	Splashdown	Purchased
Feb. 28	King Merlin	Second
March 4	**Probably's Halo**	**Third**
March 12	King Merlin	Third
March 13	**Probably's Halo**	**Third**
March 29	King Merlin	Second
March 29	**Probably's Halo**	**Sixth**
April 26	King Merlin	Won
May 2	Wishing Star	Claimed
May 24	King Merlin	Won
June 3	Wishing Star	Seventh, claimed
June 14	King Merlin	Seventh
June 14	Splashdown	Fourth
June 14	Me Last Dance	Claimed
July 10	King Merlin	Sixth
July 28	Splashdown	Fifth

July 29	King Merlin	Won, claimed
Aug. 6	**Hampshire Dancer**	**Second**
Aug. 9	Me Last Dance	Claimed
Aug. 12	Splashdown	Sixth
Aug. 16	Eastern Glow	Claimed
Aug. 23	**Hampshire Dancer**	**Third**
Sept. 3	Eastern Glow	Won
Sept. 14	**Hampshire Dancer**	**Won**
Sept. 20	Splashdown	Won
Oct. 3	Splashdown	Third
Oct. 10	Splashdown	Second
Oct. 11	**Hampshire Dancer**	**Eleventh**
Nov. 3	Eastern Glow	Won
Dec. 4	Eastern Glow	Seventh
Dec. 26	Eastern Glow	Fifth
Dec. 31	**Probably's Halo**	**Tenth, claimed**

1999

Jan. 1	**Hampshire Dancer**	**Third**
Jan. 15	Eastern Glow	Third
Jan. 29	Eastern Glow	Second, claimed
Jan. 29	**Hampshire Dancer**	**Third**

Feb. 11	**Hampshire Dancer**	**Second**
Feb. 25	**Hampshire Dancer**	**Fifth**
Feb. 27	Indian Sprout	Ninth
Feb. 27	Eastern Glow	Claimed
March 3	Mister D	Claimed
March 5	Indian Sprout	Eighth
March 12	Eastern Glow	Fifth
March 19	Eastern Glow	Second, claimed
April 8	Mister D	Fourth
May 1	Mister D	Second
May 19	**Hampshire Dancer**	**Fourth**
May 28	Mister D	Second, claimed
June 4	**Hampshire Dancer**	**Fourth**
June 16	**Hampshire Dancer**	**Fourth**
July 2	**Hampshire Dancer**	**Third**
July 3	Illegal Motion	Claimed
July 4	Indian Sprout	Won
July 21	Indian Sprout	Second, claimed
July 29	**Hampshire Dancer**	**Won**
July 29	Illegal Motion	Second
Aug. 22	Illegal Motion	Fifth
Aug. 27	Greek Mythology	Claimed

Sept. 3	Illegal Motion	Won, claimed
Sept. 10	Barley Creek	Claimed
Sept. 19	**Hampshire Dancer**	**Seventh**
Sept. 27	**Hampshire Dancer**	**Fifth**
Nov. 21	Barley Creek	Sixth
Dec. 2	Barley Creek	Sixth, claimed
Dec. 9	Greek Mythology	Fourth
Dec. 12	**Hampshire Dancer**	**Third**
Dec. 27	Flying Affair	Claimed
Dec. 31	Greek Mythology	Seventh

2000

Jan. 5	Flying Affair	Claimed
Feb. 5	Valley Run	Claimed
March 2	Valley Run	Won
March	16 Valley Run	Fourth
March 26	Valley Run	Won, claimed
March 31	My Boy C K	Claimed
April 5	Rammer	Claimed
April 16	My Boy C K	Won
April 26	Rammer	Second
April 29	My Boy C K	Third

May 3	Song Dynasty	Claimed
May 13	My Boy C K	Fifth
May 19	Rammer	Second
May 26	Song Dynasty	Fourth, claimed
June 16	Rammer	Seventh
June 23	My Boy C K	Won
June 23	Launch the Quest	Claimed
July 21	Oskaloosa	Claimed
July 22	Style master	Claimed
July 22	St. Mo	Claimed
July 24	My Boy C K	Fourth
Aug. 4	Oskaloosa	Sixth, retired
Aug. 12	St. Mo	Sixth
Aug. 23	Launch the Quest	Won
Aug. 26	My Boy C K	Sixth, retired
Aug. 29	**Probably's Devil**	**Won**
Sept. 8	St. Mo	Fifth
Sept. 11	Launch the Quest	Seventh
Sept. 12	Winalotalace	Claimed
Oct. 2	Launch the Quest	Retired
Oct. 4	**Probably's Devil**	**Won**
Oct. 9	Winalotalace	Second

Oct. 18	**Probably's Devil**	**Second**
Nov. 11	Winalotalace	Sixth, claimed
Nov. 16	**Probably's Devil**	**Second**
Nov. 30	Coquinta Bay	Claimed
Dec. 17	Coquinta Bay	Third
Dec. 26	Coquinta Bay	Won
Dec.	26 Rammer	Fourth

2001

Jan. 12	Rammer	Won
Jan. 19	Coquinta Bay	Won
Jan. 26	Coquinta Bay	Sixth
Feb. 15	Coquinta Bay	Third
Feb. 21	Rammer	Fifth
March 2	Coquinta Bay	Won, claimed
March 2	Rammer	Won
March 4	Grand Picken	Claimed
March 7	Hampshire Dancer	Second
March 21	Grand Picken	Won, claimed
April 1	Rammer	Fifth
April 1	Grand Picken	Claimed
April 13	**Hampshire Dancer**	**Fourth**

April 20	Grand Picken	Third
April 26	**Hampshire Dancer**	**Third**
April 26	Redliner	Claimed
April 28	Rammer	Second
May 5	Redliner	Fourth
May 5	Mac's Ghost	Second
May 13	Rammer	Third, claimed
May 16	Grand Picken	Fourth, claimed
May 17	Redliner	Won, claimed
May 17	**Hampshire Dancer**	**Fourth**
May 22	Carney's Princess	Claimed
June 8	Mac's Ghost	Second
June 8	Carney's Princess	Fifth
June 15	Redliner	Claimed
June 17	**Hampshire Dancer**	**Fourth**
June 17	Carney's Princess	Fourth, claimed
June 30	Mac's Ghost	Second
July 4	**Hampshire Dancer**	**Eighth**
July 9	Redliner	Fourth
July 13	**Hampshire Dancer**	**Won**
July 18	Redliner	Seventh
July 25	Mac's Ghost	Won, claimed

July 29	**Hampshire Dancer**	**Fifth**
Aug. 11	**Probably's Devil**	**Ninth**
Aug. 24	**Hampshire Dancer**	**Won**
Sept. 1	**Probably's Devil**	**Won**
Sept. 17	Forlabid	Claimed
Sept. 26	**Probably's Devil**	**Second**
Oct. 10	**Probably's Devil**	**Won**
Oct. 17	Gold Comet	Fifth
Oct. 17	Fleet Queen	Claimed
Nov. 7	Forlabid	Ninth
Nov. 16	Gold Comet	Sixth
Nov. 26	Gold Comet	Fifth
Nov. 25	Fleet Queen	Won
Dec. 8	Fleet Queen	Fifth
Dec. 30	Gold Comet	Fourth

2002

Jan. 6	Fleet Queen	Fifth
Jan. 18	Fleet Queen	Won
Jan. 29	Fleet Queen	Fifth, claimed
May 5	Pohatan Princess	Claimed
May 25	Dronero	Claimed

June 8	Pohatan Princess	Won
July 6	Dronero	Won
July 12	Pohatan Princess	Fourth
July 26	Dronero	Won
Aug. 4	Pohatan Princess	Fifth
Aug. 14	Dronero	Fourth
Aug. 20	Pohatan Princess	Fifth
Sept. 3	Dronero	Sixth
Sept. 21	Pohatan Princess	Won, claimed
Oct. 11	Dronero	Sixth
Oct. 14	Pick Me Buzz	Claimed
Nov. 15	Dronero	Won
Nov. 27	Pick Me Buzz	Won
Dec. 1	Little Miss Hurry	Claimed
Dec. 4	Dronero	Ninth
Dec. 12	Pick Me Buzz	Won
Dec. 19	Little Miss Hurry	Fifth
Dec. 29	Pick Me Buzz	Second

2003

Jan. 2	Dronero	Third
Jan. 4	Pick Me Buzz	Won

Jan. 22	Dronero	Fifth
Jan. 27	Landler	Claimed
Jan. 30	Little Miss Hurry	Fourth
Jan. 30	Pick Me Buzz	Third
March 6	Dronero	Third
March 7	Landler	Won
March 13	Little Miss Hurry	Eighth
March 19	Pick Me Buzz	Eighth
March 19	Landler	Second
March 27	Little Miss Hurry	Retired
April 2	Pick Me Buzz	Second
April 3	Dronero	Sixth
April 6	OK With Me	Sixth, claimed
April 26	Pick Me Buzz	Fifth
May 2	Landler	Won
May 17	Landler	Won
May 19	Pick Me Buzz	Fifth, claimed
May 24	King of Swing	Claimed
June 5	Landler	Second
June 18	King of Swing	Second, claimed
June 28	Landler	Won
June 28	King of Swing	Claimed

July 19	Landler	Won
July 19	King of Swing	Tenth
Aug. 6	Landler	Second
Aug. 24	King of Swing	Retired
Sept. 4	Landler	Won
Sept. 9	Killer Angel	Claimed
Sept. 29	Killer Angel	Fourth
Oct. 13	Killer Angel	Fourth
Oct. 25	**Probably's Devil**	**Fifth**
Oct. 25	Lucky Ticket	Claimed
Oct. 29	Killer Angel	Fifth
Nov. 2	Mercy Ridge	Claimed
Nov. 8	**Probably's Devil**	**Fifth**
Nov. 14	Lucky Ticket	Tenth, claimed
Nov. 14	Killer Angel	Third, claimed
Dec. 3	**Probably's Devil**	**Fourth**
Dec. 20	Mercy Ridge	Won
Dec. 31	Nicelittlepackage	Claimed

2004

| **Jan. 3** | **Probably's Devil** | **Eighth** |
| Jan. 4 | Mercy Ridge | Fifth |

Jan. 22	**Probably's Devil**	**Fifth**
Feb. 15	Nicelittlepackage	Second
Feb. 20	Norton Street	Third
March 3	Nicelittlepackage	Won
March 10	Norton Street	Won, claimed
March 19	**Probably's Devil**	**Seventh**
March 27	Nicelittlepackage	Second
April 16	Probably's Devil	Second
April 28	Nicelittlepackage	Won, claimed
May 8	Vif	Claimed
May 10	**Probably's Devil**	**Sixth, retired**
May 31	Landler	Won
June 3	Action Attraction	Claimed
June 6	Vif	Seventh
June 19	Landler	Fourth
June 30	Three Aces	Sixth
July 2	Action Attraction	Second, claimed
July 9	Deseo	Claimed
July 16	Three Aces	Ninth
July 16	Lucky Larue	Claimed
July 18	Landler	Third
July 31	Landler	Sixth
Sept. 3	Deseo	Won

Sept. 5	Three Aces	Second
Sept. 10	Lucky Larue	Second
Sept. 11	Steady Stream	Claimed
Oct. 11	Sinking Feeling	Claimed
Oct. 16	Deseo	Eighth, pulled up
Oct. 21	Three Aces	Won
Oct. 22	Deseo	Won
Oct. 23	Steady Stream	Fourth
Oct. 23	Lucky Larue	Third, retired
Oct. 29	Sinking Feeling	Third
Nov. 7	Deseo	Fourth
Nov. 10	Three Aces	Seventh
Nov. 14	Steady Stream	Ninth
Nov. 12	Unaccounted Affair	Claimed
Nov. 22	Moon Lust	Seventh
Nov. 27	Deseo	Third, claimed
Dec. 10	Steady Stream	Second
Dec. 21	Three Aces	Won

2005

Jan. 15	Steady Stream	Third
Feb. 2	Steady Stream	Eighth
Feb. 16	Steady Stream	Second

Feb. 25	Three Aces	Won
March 18	Steady Stream	Second
March 19	Landler	Sixth
March 31	Moon Lust	Ninth
April 2	Steady Stream	Third
April 20	Moon Lust	Tenth
April 29	Landler	Won, claimed
May 22	Karate Kat	Fourth
May 29	Three Aces	Seventh
June 9	Karate Kat	Fifth
June 10	Three Aces	Third
July 16	Karate Kat	Won
July 28	Three Aces	Third
Aug. 7	Karate Kat	Won
Sept. 15	Three Aces	Eighth
Sept. 17	Karate Kat	Second
Oct. 8	Karate Kat	Fifth
Oct. 8	Three Aces	Third
Oct. 14	**Lunar Indian**	**Second**
Nov. 6	**Lunar Indian**	**Won**
Nov. 26	Karate Kat	Third
Dec. 2	Karate Kat	Fourth

Dec. 10	Moon Lust	Retired
Dec. 11	Three Aces	Won
Dec. 28	Isn't True	Claimed

2006

Jan. 12	Isn't True	Fifth
Jan. 21	Lovely Countess	Second
Jan. 26	Isn't True	Sixth
Feb. 25	Isn't True	Ninth, retired
Feb. 25	Pay Your Taxes	Sixth
March 3	Lovely Countess	Fourth
March 5	Double Tollgate	Won

Bold face: horses bred by Hampshire breeding partnerships

THE HAMPSHIRE
RECORD BY YEAR

1989

Races	Won	Place	Show	Fourth
31	7	1	4	3

1990

39	6	9	7	4
(70)	(13)	(10)	(11)	(7)

1991

66	14	8	8	9
(136)	(27)	(18)	(19)	(16)

1992

41	8	6	8	7
(177)	(35)	(24)	(27)	(23)

1993

| 43 | 11 | 5 | 3 | 6 |
| (220) | (46) | (29) | (30) | (29) |

1994

| 4 | 1 | 0 | 1 | 0 |
| (224) | (47) | (29) | (31) | (29) |

1995

| 24 | 4 | 4 | 2 | 4 |
| (248) | (51) | (33) | (33) | (33) |

1996

| 21 | 4 | 0 | 4 | 0 |
| (269) | (55) | (33) | (37) | (33) |

1997

| 27 | 3 | 2 | 2 | 4 |
| (296) | (58) | (35) | (39) | 5 (37) |

1998

| 32 | 7 | 4 | 6 | 5 |
| (328) | (65) | (39) | (45) | (38) |

1999

| 41 | 4 | 9 | 6 | 9 |
| (369) | (69) | (48) | (51) | (47) |

187

2000

30	8	5	2	4
(399)	(77)	(53)	(53)	(51)

2001

44	13	6	4	8
(443)	(90)	(59)	(57)	(59)

2002

19	8	1	0	2
(462)	(98)	(60)	(57)	(61)

2003

34	8	5	4	4
(496)	(106)	(65)	(61)	(65)

2004

37	7	7	5	3
(533)	(114)	(72)	(66)	(68)

2005

26	6	5	4	4
(559)	(120)	(77)	(70)	(72)

WIN, ON-THE-BOARD
PERCENTAGES BY YEAR

1989 - 23% win, 48% on-the-board

1990 - 15% win, 66% on-the-board

1991 - 21% win, 59% on-the-board

1992 - 20% win, 71% on-the-board

1993 - 25% win, 58% on-the-board

1994 - 25% win, 50% on-the-board

1995 - 16% win, 58% on-the-board

1996 - 20% win, 58% on-the-board

1997 - 11% win, 41% on-the-board

1998 - 22% win, 68% on-the-board

1999 - 9% win, 68% on-the-board

2000 - 27% win, 63% on-the-board

2001 - 30% win, 70% on-the-board

2002 - 44% win, 60% on-the-board

2003 - 23% win, 60% on-the-board

2004 - 19% win, 60% on-the-board

2005 - 23 % win, 69% on-the-board

1989 - 2005 - 21% win, 60% on-the-board.

(For the purists, tabulating only the first three, 47% in-the-money.)

THE HAMPSHIRE'S PRINCIPAL OFFICERS

Malcolm Barr, President and Co-Founder

British-born Barr is renowned for his gift of the gab but fortunately took diction lessons to smooth out a rich Derbyshire accent baffling to even many other Britons before emigrating to the United States via Canada. He's now readily understood - most of the time.

As a far-ranging journalist, Barr worked an international beat, then joined The Associated Press in Honolulu, later moving to its Washington bureau. He served in public affairs/media management posts with the Departments of Justice, Labor and Commerce in Washington, D.C., as well as a press secretary to U.S. Senator Hiram L. Fong (R-Hawaii), retiring after 25 years government service in 1995.

He is a past president of the Wire Service Guild (AFL-CIO), a former vice-president of the Washington Press Club, and a member of the National Press Club, the Maryland Thoroughbred Horsemen's Association, the West Virginia

Thoroughbred Breeders' Association, the U.S. Marine Corps Combat Correspondents' Association, the Virginia Thoroughbred Association, and Rotary International. His community activities revolve around children and abused dogs and horses.

Barr and his wife, Carol, a former manager in the U. S. Customs Service, make their home in Front Royal, Virginia, and have a son, Malcolm, Jr., serving in the U.S. Air Force.

Bill Joyce (left) and Malcolm Barr, Sr., five years after forming the Hampshire partnerships, photographed at a symposium they organized at Belmont Park.

WILLIAM JOYCE, VICE PRESIDENT AND CO-FOUNDER

A Boston native and graduate of Georgetown University Law Center, Bill Joyce admits to a somewhat crooked start in racing. When he was eight, his father, Bill, would sneak him under the turnstiles at Wonderland Park, a dog track in Revere, Massachusetts.

Joyce served as a staff assistant in President Lyndon Johnson's White House, as an assistant U.S. attorney in Boston and Alexandria, Virginia, and as an administrative law judge in what was then the U.S Immigration and Naturalization Service. He currently is in private practice in Boston.

Joyce and his wife, Kathyrn, live in Duxbury, Massachussets. They have a daughter, Laura.

V. CAROL BARR, TREASURER

A native of Virginia and a management official with the U.S. Customs Service in its Washington, D.C. headquarters, Carol stepped up to the plate to fulfill a dual role as Treasurer and Chief Financial Officer of the Hampshire when Bill Joyce left the Mid-Atlantic thoroughbred racing area in 1996 to pursue his legal career in Massachusetts. Carol kept the books and fulfilled her treasurer's role while the Hampshire grew from 2-3 partnerships (28 share owners) owning four horses in 1996 to nine partnerships with up to 14 horses and 70 share owners in 2005. She retired in 1999 after 35 years of U.S. government service and continues to help her husband of 23 years operate the partnerships from their Front Royal, VA, home.

GLOSSARY OF TERMS

Allowance race -- A step up in class from a claiming race, a race in which your horse is *not* for sale. Also known as handicaps.

Backside -- That part of the racetrack where the barns and stalls are situated. Where your horses live.

Bloodstock agent -- A person you hire to advise on both the private purchase and sale of your horses.

Breeding partnership -- A syndicate dedicated to breeding horses, in our case specifically for racing. Others may breed for selling the weanlings and yearlings prior to racing.

Broodmare -- The female horse(s) from which we breed.

Bookkeeper -- The track bookkeeper takes your money, maintains your account at the track, issues your IRS tax form 1099s, and sometimes sends you a check.

Breezing -- See "workouts".

Claiming race -- The first and lowest racing classification, a race in which all horses are for sale to a licensed owner or trainer for a specified price.

Condition book -- The Bible of every trainer which lists every race at every meet, and the conditions of those races under which he must choose to race the horses under his charge.

Daily Racing Form -- The Bible of every serious thoroughbred handicapper.

Grooms -- Each groom may have up to a half dozen horses to feed, water, keep the stalls clean, and, well, groom.

Paddock -- Where the horses are taken before each race, and where the owners can visit to watch them being saddled, chat with the trainer and the jockey. It's all part of the racing scene.

Photographer -- The track photographer, the most important guy at the track for owners.

Purses -- What you win, when you win.

Racing partnership -- A syndicate dedicated to purchasing horses for racing.

Racing secretary -- Organizes each racing card, depending on the availability of horses in the various categories.

Stakes race -- The crème de la creme of races, the one we all strive to achieve, and to win.

Stallion barn -- Where your broodmare goes for her date with destiny.

Weanlings -- Young horses before they reach their first birthday (January 1), when they become yearlings.

Winner's circle -- Where we all congregate for photographs with our horse, the horse's trainer and jockey.

Workouts -- An official clocker must be notified in the event of a workout, the time being recorded in the *Daily Racing Form* and the racing program. Your horse must have had a workout at least once within 30 days of a race. Workouts, or breezes, are conducted during exercise time in the mornings.

Steady Stream in the stretch at Charles Town on November 14, 2004. Photo by Laurie Asseo, Hampshire partner.

ACKNOWLEDGEMENTS

First, I'd like to thank the magnificent horses...then their grooms, the unsung heroes of the industry.

Surviving for seventeen years in the claiming business would not have been possible without our principal trainer, Dale Capuano. As the magazine said, "a legend in the making." We hope we helped make the legend. And thanks to his dad, Philip, who got us into the breeding business with a one-hour lecture and a free stallion service. Thanks to Philip's brother, Louis, who saw us through our first five foals and treated their dam, Probably The One, like a daughter. Thanks to Amy Nicol for giving the mare a forever home and a dignified passage to horse heaven. Thanks to all of those who have helped provide homes for our sick, our injured, and our just plain worn out horses. We should all do as much.

Thanks to our hundreds of partners and to those few who became directors of our enterprise. Their counsel and support was invaluable. Thanks to my wife, Carol, for being a scrupulous book keeper, and to my son, Malcolm, Jr., for joining the military and allowing me to buy my own race horse. I'm proud of you, kid!

And finally, my heartfelt appreciation to my long-time newshound friend, co-author Tom Ardies, an accomplished writer who has a dozen published novels and a screenwriting credit. He lives in San Diego.

Malcolm Barr, Sr.

EPILOGUE

As we await publication of this book about the Hampshire's horses and the people who owned them, the first months of 2006 illustrated both the highest peaks and the lowest valleys that thoroughbred ownership can bestow.

The Hampshire's finest filly of 2005, Karate Kat, was retired from the track due to a serious neurological complaint; the partners' homebred, Lunar Indian, was set down, possibly for good, when the ligaments that control his front legs were seriously compromised (he is currently in enforced stall rest for an unknown period of time); top wage earner Three Aces was being treated for a back injury; and the valuable mare Lovely Countess snapped a foreleg in a race at Charles Town, WV, May 10 and was humanely euthanized on the track before reaching her full potential. This was the second on-track fatality in more than 550 races by Hampshire horses in 17-plus years, both of them at Charles Town.

Meanwhile, trainer Dale Capuano discovered that minor throat surgery was the answer to Lively Sweep's problems and he swept to victory at Pimlico on May 7th and was to be entered on the Black Eyed Susan under card prior to the Preakness on May 19th. Pay Your Taxes, now tutored by a new Charles Town trainer, Marion L. (Lyn) Cuttino, was a popular winner just after 2005 tax day (April 17th), and the partners' brood mare Oskaloosa produced a healthy foal, a colt, by Way West, on April 4. And on May 11th, Marnie's Imperial, the 3-year-old gray, West Virginia-bred filly Barr purchased with his son's college funds, was sent to Capuano for training at Laurel Park.

Landler, whose story we told in Chapter 1, continued to race successfully in 2006, at the lower ($8,000) claiming levels, but for different ownership interests. The thoughts of his Hampshire owners are with him always. Go, baby, go!

M.B.

About the Authors

For 25 years, directly out of high school in England, Malcolm Barr pursued a successful career in journalism in three countries, the United Kingdom, Canada, and the United States. This reporting odyssey ended in Washington, D.C., where he was transferred by The Associated Press from Honolulu and where he worked as a criminal justice correspondent until 1969. Barr also freelanced many magazine and newspaper articles in several countries during his journalism career. Quitting journalism for the political scene--the U.S. Senate--and government, where he worked as a public relations manager for the departments of Labor, Justice and Commerce, Barr spent a quarter century in a second career in Washington. While at the U.S. Department of Justice, Barr headed the team that led to the launching of McGruff, the familiar anti-crime icon, and wrote the original support materials for the McGruff program. He supervised the contest that named the dog, introducing the New Orleans police officer who named him at a National Press Club ceremony in 1980. A popular feature of the Hampshire racing partnerships is the monthly newsletter that Barr has written and edited for partners for the past 17 years. Barr is retired and lives in Front Royal, Va.

Tom Ardies, a former newspaperman with the Vancouver (Canada) Sun and the Honolulu Star-Bulletin, is a successful novelist living in San Diego, CA.

Printed in the United States
101402LV00006B/3/A